Praise for *Sacred Tears*

"Weber's voice serves as an intimate gu.... underbrush of grief. This book resonates with the authenticity that can only come from someone who has known loss as a witch knows the earth—deeply and reverently. ... Weber doesn't just share her journey and insight; she provides tangible anchors such as spells, rituals, prayers, and exercises designed to foster healing, enable grieving, channel justifiable rage into constructive action, and maintain a sacred connection with those we've lost ... *Sacred Tears* stands as a source of solace and kinship for those dealing with grief."

—**MAT AURYN**, international bestselling author of *Psychic Witch*

"Weber wrote *Sacred Tears*, a book filled with wisdom, practical advice, spells, and more, for those of us who need support but don't follow a mainstream spiritual path. ... While there are plenty of books on the topic of grief, none aligned with my spiritual practice. Courtney's personal stories are heart-wrenching, but they help connect her story to the practices—and to us, the readers and members of the witchcraft community."

—**THERESA REED**, author of *The Cards You're Dealt: How to Deal When Life Gets Real*

"Once in a great while, a book comes along at just the right time. *Sacred Tears* is that book. Between its covers readers will find wisdom, authority, vulnerability, and courage. Amidst the helpful mix there are unique takeaways in the form of rituals, stories, and practices. This book is significant and much needed. Get it, read it and gift it—use it to ease one of our most challenging passages of life."

—**PRIESTESS STEPHANIE ROSE BIRD**, author of *Sticks, Stones, Roots and Bones, African American Magick,* and *Motherland Herbal*

"Words are magic and Witches know that when they need it, the right book always arrives. With compassion and hard-earned wisdom, Courtney has transmuted her own deep grief into a gift for all who are suffering the sorrows of loss. She offers wise words and heartfelt rites to help us grow larger hearts around the holes that are inevitable when we love."

—**PHYLLIS CUROTT,** author of *Book of Shadows*, *The Witches Wisdom Tarot*, and *Spells for Living Well*

"This is the book I wish I had when my father died. It's raw, poignant, sensitive, and most importantly, the magic in here works!"

—**DEVIN HUNTER,** author of *Modern Witch*

"Weber has done a phenomenal job of sharing her personal pain and journey through grief, while opening a portal for us to heal when sadness and loss seep into our lives through the passing of loved ones or the end of beloved relationships."

—**NAJAH LIGHTFOOT,** author of *Good Juju* and *Powerful Juju*

"Weber connects with vulnerability and her deep Witch wisdom. She shares what she's been through in words, both powerful and raw. … She takes your hand to guide you through spells and rituals to process, acknowledge, heal, and then stand strong in your own power. *Sacred Tears* is a treasure of a book that helps us to process and honor grief as Witches."

—**VERONICA VARLOW,** author of *Bohemian Magick*

"Weber hits right in the heart with the very real, raw, and unfiltered emotions that surround grief. Her words have an incredible way of making you feel that she's sitting you down, holding your hand, and giving you a much-needed and sincere metaphorical hug. *Sacred Tears* is truly a heartfelt gift and an incredible guide."

—**LAURA TEMPEST ZAKROFF,** author of *Weave the Liminal*

SACRED
TEARS

About the Author

Courtney Weber is a priestess, Witch, writer, tarot advisor, and teacher. She is the creator of *Tarot of the Boroughs* and the author of *Hekate*, *The Morrigan*, *Brigid*, and *Tarot for One*. She is also a contributor to *Cancer Witch* and a cohost of *That Witch Life* podcast. Visit her at CourtneyAWeber.com.

SACRED TEARS

A Witch's Guide to Grief

foreword by CHRISTOPHER PENCZAK

COURTNEY WEBER

Llewellyn Publications
Woodbury, Minnesota

FIRST EDITION
First Printing, 2024

Book design by Christine Ha
Cover design by Verlynda Pinckney
Tarot card illustrations are based on those contained in *The Pictorial Key to the Tarot* by Arthur Edward Waite, published by William Rider & Son Ltd., London 1911.

Llewellyn Publications is a registered trademark of Llewellyn Worldwide Ltd.

Library of Congress Cataloging-in-Publication Data (Pending)
ISBN: 978-0-7387-7631-6

Llewellyn Worldwide Ltd. does not participate in, endorse, or have any authority or responsibility concerning private business transactions between our authors and the public.

All mail addressed to the author is forwarded but the publisher cannot, unless specifically instructed by the author, give out an address or phone number.

Any internet references contained in this work are current at publication time, but the publisher cannot guarantee that a specific location will continue to be maintained. Please refer to the publisher's website for links to authors' websites and other sources.

Llewellyn Publications
A Division of Llewellyn Worldwide Ltd.
2143 Wooddale Drive
Woodbury, MN 55125-2989
www.llewellyn.com

Printed in the United States of America

Other Books by Courtney Weber

Hekate: Goddess of Witches

The Morrigan: Celtic Goddess of Magick and Might

Tarot for One: The Art of Reading for Yourself

Brigid: History, Mystery, and Magick of the Celtic Goddess

Tarot of the Boroughs

Cancer Witch (Contributor)

Note

Sacred Tears is intended to provide spiritual support and general information on the process of grief. It is not a substitute for medical or psychological treatment and may not be relied upon for the purposes of diagnosing or treating any condition or illness. Please seek out the care of a professional healthcare provider if you are experiencing symptoms of any potentially serious condition.

For Ripley

Contents

Rituals, Prayers, and Practices

Foreword

The magick is in the living of things. I know we think of magick— and by extension, Witchcraft—as the spells and potions, the rituals, and the displays of psychic abilities, but the true magick is in the living of life, in the everyday and ordinary things everyone experiences. Magick is in the things we take for granted. This includes the little things, events we sail through every day often without much thought, like cooking, cleaning, and our daily work. The bigger things, we try not to give much thought to, until they happen to us.

While cataclysmic to us and our loved ones, the big, scary, awful life changes of sickness, injury, and death are really part of the ordinary and everyday. They might not happen to us every day, but they happen every day to someone, to many someones, and their waves ripple out and affect us all. They are ordinary in the sense that they are the natural and expected results of life. While the circumstances can seem unfair, we know from our experience they are part of life. What is a life gone too soon? We know there is no way to know for certain when a life will end, but we have come to expect long and healthy lives in our modern world. Still, there is no promise of it, and we see examples of such loss all the time, but most of us like to think it won't happen to us and our loved ones. Until it does.

I think often of a quote from one my favorite authors, through the character of Death. At various times, she (Death) tells those whose lives are at an end that they experienced what everyone else does: a lifetime.[1]

By "ordinary" and "everyday," I certainly do not mean such experiences lack meaning because they happen so frequently. Quite the contrary: they are part of the very fabric of life, as fundamental to our universe as gravity and electromagnetism, or to our environment as weather and seasons. Illness, injury, loss, and death are as much fundamental building blocks as birth, life, health, and harvest.

As a Witch and a teacher of Witchcraft, I speak a lot about harvest, sacrifice, death, and rebirth, as many other Witches do. We see the modern regeneration of our practice as having roots in the magick and medicine of the agrarian cycle and the folkloric village life many of us in the modern world romanticize. We tend to forget how much work it was, and still is, for those living that way, and that in such times the line between life and death was often finer, the safety net of society less secure. A bad harvest could equal real deaths. While I talk about it, I am also distant from it in my nice, safe house. I, too, think that could never happen to me.

---

1. Neil Gaiman, Sam Kieth, Mike Dringenberg, Malcolm Jones III, Daniel Vozzo, Todd Klein, *The Sandman, vol. 1: Preludes & Nocturnes* (New York: DC Comics, 2010).

Yet history shows us time and again that, yes, it could happen to me. It could happen to any of us.

Because of this, a lot of Witches are more distant from death than we like to pretend we are. True, many of us contemplate and meditate on death, do spirit work to commune with the ancestors, and even engage in mediumship to connect to the recently deceased, and that certainly helps us integrate our spiritual understanding of death and renewal. But it's a few steps away from death itself. Some fetishize death and darkness, and while I think the macabre aesthetic has its place in our tradition, it must be done with more awareness than simply a fashion choice. Like some Eastern traditions of India and Tibet, where practices may take place in crematoriums or use icons of skulls and wrathful divinities, these rites help us know the reality of these forces as a natural part of the cosmos. Few of us will ever understand these realities. Since we cannot overcome this reality, some of us look to darkness and death to empower ourselves with (and sometimes over) others when starting on the path. Embracing such iconography for that reason might help us over an initial hurdle but will challenge us to really understand and embrace the true darker mysteries. So, when death shows up, it can surprise and even stun us, even when we think we are in relationship with death, through walking side by side with ancestors and underworld deities.

As a Witch, I consider myself a part of a priesthood, though I realize not all who identify with the word *Witch* do so. From my experience, we learn to be our own priests to conduct personal rituals for ourselves and a small group of peers, and then can learn the greater mysteries of teaching, leading, healing, and ministering in forms of high priesthood, or clergy. Today, support for the clergy side of Paganism and Witchcraft is growing, and we take on many roles that our magickal training did not prepare us to face.

One such role is sitting with the dying and ministering to the family of the recently deceased. While any academic study can be helpful, nothing really prepares you for it until you do it, and even then, each time is wholly unique. Everyone needs something different, and everyone responds to your presence differently. Sometimes it's simple silence and presence. Sometimes it's talking about beliefs and paradigms of the afterlife. Other times, it's ritual, meditation, or energy work. For me, it has been about sitting and being fully present.

As a Witch, you sometimes get called to minister to people who don't fit into any other religion or spiritual paradigm. We provide rituals of crossing for the spirit and funerary rites for the family and community. Often, one ritual can serve both purposes. But beyond that, we don't have a lot of resources, support, or teachings to take you further. That is thankfully changing, but that is why I empathize deeply with Courtney's feelings toward our shared practices in Witchcraft. I have been there myself in different ways. I know that she, too, as a teacher, community leader, and healer, has had similar foundations and responsibilities in community. When I look back on what training I had, there was little to address the priest or minister of the Craft when going through their own grief process. There are some strange expectations that grief shouldn't be a big deal for a "spiritual leader" and no support is necessary.

Magick often manifests in profound inner and outer awareness. You are in the right place at the right time, doing the right thing. The worlds align, and something happens. It's not always outwardly big, but as you grow in your Craft, you find it's the inwardly big, outwardly subtle things that carry the most magick. At least, they do for me.

Unbeknownst to her, on the anniversary of my mother's death, May third, I received a message from Courtney about this book, *Sacred Tears*. Though it has been many years, death and life and family were on my mind. The call was an aligning of worlds. Something opened in me and said yes despite just previously telling my partners how busy my coming schedule was and having little time for anything else. If the message came a day later or a day earlier, my response might have been different. But at that moment, I didn't need any further sign. Magick was afoot.

My mother's passing—her initial diagnosis of pancreatic cancer, struggles, surgeries, chemotherapy and radiation, explorations into alternative medicine, and eventual death—was one of the biggest gifts she could give her loved ones. Also a Witch, we were lucky to have both the time to talk and a mutual understanding of beliefs, hopes, fears, and disappointments. Nothing was left unsaid. As a Witch, she brought the mystery of illness, sacrifice, death, and grief into my life. It was no longer as distant and would never be again. While grief is a process, it never quite goes away. Your relationship to it changes with time, magick, and awareness. I might not be taking in the harvest or the hunt as my Pagan ancestors did, with life hanging in the balance and death a clear possibility, but death is clearly with me now, and it helps frame my actions and understanding, and strangely, some sense of greater peace. Each death since then has brought different experiences and understanding, and just because I feel their presence continually doesn't mean those deaths were easy. In fact, perhaps understanding death and grief better, they were a bit harder, yet also gifts. That blessing and blasting that death can simultaneously be, like the blessing and blasting of the Witch, is the magickal paradox where the deep truth is both and neither. When the worlds align, the synchronicities happen, and life is lived—that is when the magick is truly expressed. You chose this book. Read it. When the time is right, try things. Let things shift. See what happens.

I am deeply proud to read such a level of raw honesty and deep sharing in this text, though I would really expect nothing less from Courtney. She is a remarkable priestess who inspires me. That level of sharing can help us know we are not alone in our grief and pain, and sometimes that is the most important part. I am excited to see her adding more to the growing ways Witches, Pagans, or anyone magickally minded can navigate their way in grief.

Know that death comes for all of us, and despite the enormity of it, it is also a natural, ordinary thing: a part of life. Embrace the enormity. Embrace the ordinary. Be with and experience whatever shows up. Look to wisdom to guide you when you can, and follow your own crooked path.

Christopher Penczak
May 2023
Salem, NH

Introduction

Hello. Welcome.

You picked up this book for a reason, and that reason surely hurt. I don't know what you've gone through. I may not even know you. It doesn't matter. I'm glad you're here. I'm sorry for the reason.

Perhaps you, too, have lost someone close to you to death or distance or a cruel disease that eclipses memory and personality. You may be navigating the loss of a relationship, platonic or romantic. Maybe a job or project you loved is no longer available, or a cause that impassioned you changed course. Maybe you're dealing with a nebulous grief, a sorrow hard to pin down, perhaps related to a changing world that won't ever be as it was again. No matter your story, I assume you are grieving.

Maybe, like me, you identify as a Witch. Perhaps you don't personally identify as a Witch, but someone you love does, and they are grieving. Maybe the whole notion of Witchcraft is new to you, but in your own grief journey, you are looking at different ways to navigate your grief. No matter your story, you are welcome here. We'll return to what it might mean to be a Witch in the first chapter. In the meantime, let's talk about loss and grief.

Loss is, unfortunately, part of life, and grief is its inevitable companion. But whether your loss happened in a moment or after a slow decline, grief remains long after whatever we loved is gone. Grief is a product of loss. It is also a product of love.

This wasn't a book I wanted to write. I experienced a loss— a kind that reshapes heart, vision, words, and worlds. It wasn't my first loss, and it certainly won't be my last, but it left me grappling for a resource that could help me, as a Witch, process what I'd experienced. The bookstores offered plenty of resources written by kind Christians, reflective Buddhists, and thoughtful, spiritual nonreligious folks, but nothing by Witches, for Witches. I craved a text that spoke to my own spiritual path. This was the book I wanted to read while I was navigating grief. Since I couldn't find that book, I wrote it.

This book does not glorify any religion or spiritual path. Nor is it an attempt to create a universal grieving system for Witches. While I share my frustrations with Witchcraft's spiritual shortcomings, it's not meant to devalue or "debunk" Witchcraft. I do share how Witchcraft has helped me through various incarnations of grief, but this book isn't a testament to the glories of Witchcraft either. This book is meant to be a companion for Witches on a journey of grief.

Many Witches describe embracing their path (aka "coming out of the broom closet") as akin to running from an oppressive society, where they perhaps felt prevented from speaking, dressing, thinking, or feeling in a way authentic to them. Some liken their embrace of Witchcraft as fleeing captivity to a lush forest, where none of the rules that contained them apply. In this proverbial forest, there is no road map and therefore no rules except those that come from the soil, air, sun, and rain. The earth, not human opinion, is in control. Instead of the constraints of arbitrary human thoughts and judgments, the Witch is linked to an ancient rhythm of the planet.

Most Witches do not live in a wild environment, yet many describe their exit from the religious or spiritual containers of their youth and entry into Witchcraft in a similar manner. There is peace in such freedom. For a time.

The untamed wild offers freedom. But it does not offer instructions or support should a solo explorer fall and break a leg. Likewise, Witchcraft offers the seeker a freedom more often denied in structured religious or spiritual traditions, but it does not always offer a path when the seeker is hurt by loss. Some might argue that no traditions offer a helpful road map for such times as these.

Maybe this is where you find yourself now.

Imagine me finding you alone and injured in this metaphorical forest in the wake of your loss. I am not a doctor or an all-purpose healer, but I have a few elixirs in my bag that helped me when I was hurt. Some of them might alleviate enough of your symptoms to help you find your way to someone else's elixir, which might alleviate a few more. Grief is deeply subjective, and there is no cure-all. It would be a mistake to expect or assume that such a cure exists. My journeys through grief have each been deeply unique, and each have required different ways of navigating them. Losing friends in a car accident was different than losing a relationship to circumstance, a beloved forest to climate change, a community to time, my first child to faulty chromosomes, and my second child to reasons I'll never know. My journeys are different from your journey. You won't agree with me on everything in this book. You're not supposed to.

Once more for the Witches in the back! You won't agree with me on everything in this book. You. Are. Not. Supposed. To.

Grief is too personal for any two stories to fully match. But hopefully you will find enough familiarity within my stories and methods to support you as you develop your own tools for navigating your loss.

I'm not alone, and neither are you. No living person is immune to loss. At present, we are collectively witnessing environmental apocalypse, mourning the loss of distinct seasons, animals, and natural spaces. Here in the United States, we are greeted nearly daily with the news of mass shootings and the deaths of persons of color at the hands of police and racism. Globally, we are experiencing rampant and violent transphobia, homophobia, Islamophobia, anti-Semitism, and a dire threat to the democracies many of us have taken for granted. As I write this, we are entering the third year of the pandemic, which has claimed nearly seven million lives globally. We are living in a time of collective grief. Witches have a special reverence for life and death, but our communities and traditions can lack the tools to navigate the grief that accompanies loss.

The Witchcraft path is deeply personal. Grief, too, is deeply personal. Grieving as a Witch is uniquely personal as well. I can't abolish your grief, but I can be your companion.

All grief has a story. Your grief has a story. The first chapter of this book includes one of my loss stories, when I lost a child twelve weeks into a pregnancy. It's harsh, gritty, and ugly, and I deliberately don't spare the details. Throughout the book, I also include stories from friends in the Witchcraft world who have experienced different types of loss, who offer different perspectives (content warning for reference to suicide in one contribution).

Social media is full of glossed-over images of grief, with ubiquitous memes encouraging sentiments such as "Don't cry because it's over … smile because it happened" and "Everything happens for a reason." I've deliberately cast aside such gloss here, which was a large part of the impetus for writing this book.

Take your time with this book. Skip some parts. Stay longer with others. Come back to the parts you skipped. It won't all be sad. Grief is full of strange and wonderful things. Some are beautiful. Others are joyful. Occasionally, grief is even funny. This doesn't mean a loss is ever "worth it." There are many gifts of grief that I would gladly give back in exchange for what I've lost. Still, one gift of grief is the opportunity to explore places within ourselves we might never see otherwise. Just as there are beautiful things that can flourish in dark places, like mushrooms and beetles and shade-loving flowers, there are parts of our souls that flourish only in the darkest times. Since we're here, we might as well look at those flourishing parts of ourselves, the beautiful things thriving in difficult times.

1

When Loss Happens

In my right arm, an IV fed painkillers into my bloodstream. On my left hand, a red-lit clip tracked my heart rate. A purple octopus crawled across the ceiling. I laughed. When I closed my eyes, I was at a cocktail party with people from another century where everyone laughed with me. I knew the octopus wasn't real but a hallucination courtesy of the drugs. I wasn't sure about the people at the party, though. They seemed real. I laughed with them until a bell screamed and my husband called my name, as my dropping heart rate had triggered an alarm. The two chalky pills the emergency room nurse told me to hold between my cheeks and gumline were finally dissolving, bitter and hateful—the medications that would hasten my body's release of the remains of our child, whose heart suddenly stopped some days before. Our doctor, a young army veteran with crisp, military elocution, dimmed the lights for my comfort.

Elsewhere in the ward, a patient experiencing an episode triggered by mental illness fought the staff. It was three a.m., my Witching hour.

Earlier that week, my book on Hekate had been released. Unbeknownst to me that night, my phone lit up with Instagram notifications and congratulatory texts. People loved the book. It changed their lives and affirmed their path, I would later read in the comments and messages. My words gave many comfort, they said. My work was leading people to Hekate.

But while that praise was coming in, I turned to my husband from my hospital bed and said, "Fuck the gods."

Maybe parts of my story sound familiar.

The moment of loss is surreal. Is it really happening? We search for clues that maybe this is all a terrible dream. We pinch ourselves or look at clocks, trying to wake from an experience that simply can't be real. It just *can't*. It can feel so unreal that we feel outside ourselves, watching this terrible thing happen to us rather than experiencing it in the moment. It couldn't be happening to us. This kind of loss is what happens to other people. Except it didn't. Our loss happened to us.

Why?

Aren't we Witches whose powers should have prevented this from happening? Did our protection spells fail? Were we cursed by an enemy? Where were the gods, guiding spirits, and ancestors? Were they asleep at the wheel? Did they cause this for some cruel, unknowable reason? Were they ever there at all?

If you are like me, you had deep questions about your religion of origin, questions that largely went away when you embraced the Witchcraft path. Witchcraft felt more real, provided more concrete experiences with a divine power, and certainly shaped life with greater purpose than the religion originally presented to us (or forced on us). But loss shatters surety, and many of us find ourselves faced with doubts, questions, and feelings of betrayal we experienced in those original religions.

What now?

Step Back in Time with Me for a Moment...

I grew up Catholic in secular Oregon. Our family was one of the few I knew who attended Mass, and of the Mass-going families, we were one of the few that attended most Sundays (not just on holidays). I did five years in Catholic school and attended CCD classes on cold, rainy Wednesday nights. I ate fish on Fridays, left room for the Holy Spirit (mostly) at school dances, and received a rosary at my confirmation, which the priest agreed to bless (even though I'd managed to skip some of the preparatory sacraments). I also attended a Methodist Bible camp on the Oregon coast every summer and dutifully listened to undulating Baptist sermons when visiting family in South Carolina. I said nightly prayers. I tried not to sin. Yet, I always felt God more in the candle flames at Mass, the ocean at Bible camp, and the red clay of my gran's backyard than in any of God's so-called houses. I was more interested in exorcisms than scripture, and in stories of angels, ghosts, and demons than those of redemption. I began to believe that God was in the physical world around me, an energy on the planet more than an invisible being in the sky. I realized I had an easier time talking to the dead than to Jesus.

On my twentieth birthday, I asked myself if I might be a Witch. The question alone made me shake with joy.

I had known for years that I wasn't really a Christian. I was *something* that didn't have a name. One day I named it, and I felt at home. I was a Witch. *I was a Witch.* I kept my revelation to myself but hugged nearly everyone I saw that day, unable to verbalize the transformation and understanding in my heart. It was too wondrous, beautiful, and sacred to share. I didn't need to. I had the spirits. I had my ancestors. I had the green, living world around me. Also, I had the gods. I didn't know what that meant, but I felt I was tapping into a multifaceted version of the divine that was far more present and palpable than the versions of God I'd known as a young Christian.

Witchcraft gifted me with purpose and adventure. After college, I moved to New York City. My first few years were rocky, filled with impulsive and expensive mistakes. Yet, as my boyfriend at the time noted, I always landed on my feet. I credited my practice of Witchcraft with keeping me employed through a staggering recession and housed when many of my peers were forced to move into their parents' basements. It took me to Ireland several times. It led me to start a coven, which blossomed into one of the largest and most active Witchcraft communities in the tristate area. I found myself at tables with some of the greatest theologians and spiritual thinkers of our time. I achieved a dream of becoming an author, and I published four books, all inspired by my beliefs and experiences as a polytheistic Witch.

Amid all of that, I met my husband.

A few months prior to meeting him, I suffered what was, at the time, the biggest heartbreak of my life. I lost a relationship with a man I thought I would marry, who had also been one of my closest friends for years. Literally, one day we were talking of marriage, and the next day the relationship was over. Truly overnight, someone whose presence was foundational for me for over a decade was functionally dead, even though he was still very much alive, as we never saw or spoke to each other again after ending the relationship. When I finally stopped crying for that relationship, I knelt at the altar I'd made to the goddess Brigid and lit a candle, performing a simple but honest spell: "Lady Brigid, you know where my life partner is. I'm ready. Bring them on."

She did. Within weeks of casting that spell, I met my husband.

My husband and I are both odd pieces of humanity's jigsaw puzzle. We both struggled to fit well with others romantically and had both begun to believe we weren't cut out for long-term relationships. But when we met each other, we found immediate comfort and chemistry that quickly blossomed into love. I credited Witchcraft with bringing him into my life.

Due to a medical condition, we knew early into our relationship that having children would be a challenge. We discussed adoption, but on our honeymoon, we admitted that we wanted biological children. Immediately after, we met with fertility doctors who said we had reason to be hopeful. We got readings from trusted spiritual advisors who saw encouraging signs. We began costly hormone therapies to correct the medical condition and performed elaborate spells recommended by readers, priests, and medicine peoples. We bathed naked in icy oceans and poured expensive whiskey out on the shore. We burned candles and prayed to Brigid, telling her we were ready to be parents. After two years, when it was clear that the expensive and logistically difficult therapies failed, we cried.

We began even more intensive medical procedures and did achieve a pregnancy. But at our first ultrasound, there was no heartbeat. The sonogram only showed a tiny circle with no life within it. It's something called *blighted ovum,* but for those who want to be pregnant, a more appropriate term might be *cruel trick.* The pregnant person experiences the discomfort of early pregnancy, while knowing the body is preparing to miscarry. When miscarriage finally arrived, I clutched a fertility charm through every wave of pain. I prayed to both Brigid and the Morrigan to help me through the fifty excruciating hours it took to pass the first loss.

When I'd healed, we tried again, but after a year without another pregnancy, we started in vitro fertilization (IVF)—a far more expensive and invasive process, which involves injections several times a day, a surgical procedure under anesthesia, and days of boring bed rest, with no guarantee of success. Weekly, I drove an hour each way for acupuncture treatments with a Chinese medicine doctor famous for her success with infertility, who prescribed me bitter herbs to choke down. I continued to light candles to the gods and made daily offerings. I sacrificed alcohol, giving "my drinks" to the altar. I petitioned our ancestors to help bring along their descendant. I slept with a fertility charm tight in my fist, one that a famous Witch gifted to me, swearing that it brought children to everyone who had ever had it. Under full moons, I stood in my backyard and spoke to the spirit of our unborn child, wherever they were. "Come on now, my darling," I would whisper to the night. "You have so many people here ready to love you."

But twice the IVF treatments failed. The tiny embryos, which my doctor said looked so promising, failed to make a home in my womb.

My husband and I kept our journey largely to ourselves. People seeking fertility treatments are often treated to infuriating and unhelpful platitudes such as "just relax" or "try CBD." They're also frequently told horror stories about failed IVF treatments. They're expected to explain why they don't "just get a surrogate" or "just adopt," as if these options were "just" simpler. It's fair to mention that when we were considering adoption, we were often immediately told adoption horror stories or expected to explain why we were "taking someone else's child instead of having our own."

When you want to have children but struggle to do it, your choices rarely satisfy anyone.

The Witchcraft community is a uniquely difficult place to navigate infertility. Besides ubiquitous images of pregnant goddesses and wading through some version of a fertility holiday every few weeks, people within our community tried to help by describing visions they'd had of our child, dreams they had of me being pregnant, or well-wishes for our "spirit baby," aka, the soul of our lost pregnancy. While these sentiments were well-meant, they were rarely well-received.

Brigid is often said to be a goddess of midwives. The Morrigan, in some myths, is said to be a mother herself. Neither of them had seemed to help us, nor had the Orishas, which our Ocha-initiated friends petitioned on our behalf. I began writing a book about Hekate. My husband and I took a dark walk to the crossroads on a new moon, where I offered the book to Hekate if she would help us have a child. As is the practice with Hekate, we left a generous offering at the crossroads and turned our backs to it, not looking behind us.

It finally happened.

In many infertility circles, it's said that a positive pregnancy test is a possibility, not a promise. We had a possibility and kept our fingers crossed and our news secret until the first ultrasound. When we saw the image of our baby and heard the *whisk-whisk-whisk* of its tiny heartbeat, I cried. Six weeks later, we had a second scan. The little heartbeat was even louder, and the image of our growing baby was clear, looking like a collection of moonstones on the screen. My belly grew quickly. Our fertility doctor called our case a success and graduated us from the clinic. I pulled together a registry, my husband and I argued over names, and we started sharing our news.

Our baby was due at Imbolg, the feast day of Brigid. It was a sign to us that the gods had been with us all along. Brigid, we believed, had finally granted us a child. Surely, Hekate had a hand in it as well.

Loss has no agenda. It doesn't consider dates, holidays, timelines. Still, when it happens, it feels like a deliberate slap from the spirits, or Fates, or whatever divine we believe in. The Monday of the twelfth week of our pregnancy began without any signs of something wrong, but the evening brought sudden blood and pain, a race to the emergency room and, finally, our loss. Our ER doctor said our child must have died shortly after our last ultrasound, right when things looked so promising. The gods were either laughing at us by letting us think we were having a child and taking it away just as we finally felt comfortable, or they didn't care about us. Maybe they weren't there at all.

In the days that followed, I sat on the couch and stared at nothing. The tiny person who had so quickly shaped my world was suddenly gone. What would my world be now? It felt like nothing. There was no world without that little person.

Meanwhile, my phone continued to blink with Instagram tags, praising my new Hekate book. My words helped people connect with a goddess and find themselves as a Witch, readers said.

Good for you, I silently responded to the praise. Not for me.

Our altar sat cold and neglected. The gods were silent.

Witchcraft was suddenly meaningless.

What Makes a Witch?

The word *Witch* has meant different things to different peoples over the centuries. Historically, the term *Witch* was often something inherently negative. A Witch was someone capable of causing harm through physical or spiritual means (such as poisoning or cursing someone), or the term was used to describe someone of ill intent. In recent decades in many parts of the Western world, *Witch* has been embraced as a revolutionary term. It has embodied many things, including formal rejection of organized religion and patriarchy, love for the earth, embrace of the sacred feminine, the shattering of gender binaries, and the practice of magick.

The definition of *Witchcraft* is as varied as the people who practice it. I personally define a Witch as someone who works with magick, which would include casting spells (defined here as performing a ritualistic action rooted in the intent to create change in someone's internal or external world) or maintaining a relationship with spirits (defined here as cognizant entities who do not exist in the flesh but still move about in the world). I know many Witches for whom Witchcraft is their religion. I also know quite a few Christians, Jews, Muslims, atheists, and more who also describe themselves as Witches. If someone casts spells or communicates with spirits (or both) and calls themselves a Witch, I, too, recognize them as such, regardless of any other religious identity. At the same time, I recognize that the word *Witch* is not welcome in all cultures and contexts. There are plenty of traditions and cultures in which people practice similar things as me, but they would not call themselves a Witch. Given this perspective, I do not assign anyone the title of Witch, but if someone calls themselves a Witch, I accept them at their word.

My journey through Witchcraft has been largely polytheistic, meaning that I believe that many different gods exist. While this is common among many Witches, it is not universal among all Witches. Many Witches believe that the divine is unknowable. Others believe in a single divine force that wears different masks.

Plenty of Witches are atheists and do not believe in gods at all, and there are plenty of other Witches who believe something else altogether.

This is one of the blessings of Witchcraft. Being a Witch inherently carries the freedom of determining one's own beliefs and moral code. There is no doctrine dictating what a Witch believes, no codes of conduct, no arbitrary rules. As a Witch, I do not worry that a small infraction will doom me to eternal suffering. I don't fear that I'll make an unwitting mistake and garner a mark against me in some heavenly book or need to pay penance to a deity. But one of the hardest lessons I learned about Witchcraft is that, even with its many freedoms, it has its own great shortcomings.

In the days after our loss, I craved a place to understand. Adrift in grief, I felt abandoned by the things I'd believed in for so long. My rituals felt false, and if there was anything behind the effigies on my altars, I wanted nothing to do with it. An unofficial tenet of Witchcraft is that we have control over what happens to us. If something bad happens, we often wonder if we failed to say the right spell or formed an intention wrong. If we have a role in what has happened to us, don't we also have the power to change the outcome? Did I, as a Witch, inadvertently cause my own loss through a misuse of energy or improper disposal of negativity? Had someone cursed me and I failed to detect it? Witchcraft may lead us to believe that we have control, but loss reminds us that we do not. No spell, ritual, or prayer can give back what was taken from us once it's truly gone.

Many people tried to console me, trying to assure me that I had done nothing wrong, which only left me wondering if I had spent my entire adult life chasing a mirage. If Witchcraft didn't cause my loss but Witchcraft also couldn't prevent it, was Witchcraft even real? What was the point of being a Witch if I couldn't control my destiny?

Questioning beliefs in the wake of loss is part of the human condition, surely, but it feels terribly lonely to the human experiencing it. I scanned bookstores for something that could provide spiritual guidance. I easily found hundreds of Witchcraft books with spells for bringing love, money, and luck into my life, as well as spells for banishing misfortune or even cursing an enemy. But none of the books could help me, as a Witch, make sense of my loss. It was easy to find rituals for honoring the dead, but no practical way to support the long grief journey after losing those dead. Unable to find anything that matched my spiritual path, I reached out to the traditions I'd abandoned and some I'd never truly explored. But the Christian books all seemed to offer variations of "Bad things are part of God's plan, so stop worrying." I found myself humming an old Tori Amos song in which she rejects Jesus's plan and embraces Judas instead. The Buddhist approach to grief could be summarized as "Bad things happen. Bad things hurt. Bad things can't be prevented." Maybe I wasn't ready to hear it. I rejected that too.

I longed for a spiritual *something* that could help me process my loss, maybe something akin to the Jewish practice of shiva, the space to sit and be still in my grief, but one rooted to my own spirituality. I realized that what I longed for was a community practice around grief. Friends within the Witchcraft community sent kind words, but they also parroted, unwittingly, many of the same things the Christian books said: "The gods have a plan," "It wasn't meant to be," "Your child will always be with you."

My faith in Witchcraft crumbled further.

For the first time since I embraced Witchcraft, my spirituality didn't offer a course of direction.

From Spirit-Led to Spirit-Gutted

Many Witches describe themselves as being *spirit-led*, something that can mean trusting one's spiritual path to lead them in the best direction, as in opportunities provided by synchronicity, intuition, or following signs or omens. This may include a belief that things happen to us because they are in our highest good. That line of thinking may also include a belief that painful things happen to make space for something better. But when a loved one dies, a partner walks out, a community falls apart or rejects us, or otherwise, that belief can feel cruel. How could a world-shattering loss be part of some highest order?

People of all traditions often lean into their spirituality during times of loss and may find great comfort in it. But it's equally common for people, even deeply spiritual or devout practitioners of a faith or tradition, to struggle to connect to their beliefs when experiencing a profound loss. It can feel as though we were dancing under the soft, hypnotic lights of a club all our lives, only to have the stark, sterile overhead lights suddenly and shamelessly turned on, brutally exposing it as bare, sterile, and ugly.

In addition to the shock, horror, fury, and sorrow you may feel when your loss first happens, you may also find yourself feeling confused, disillusioned, angry, or all of the above. You may wonder if you've failed as a Witch or were ever a Witch at all. If you were truly powerful, couldn't you have prevented this? Do the gods or spirits care? Was the loss the result of a curse? Is it some kind of energetic backlash? Is Witchcraft even real?

As a grieving Witch, these are just a few of the things you may find yourself wondering. You may even feel betrayed by your path. These thoughts and feelings are normal reactions to grief, and you are not alone in having them. It is also natural to wonder why the loss happened, and it may be tempting to solve the "why." You may find yourself trying to heal your grief as quickly as possible through spells, rituals, and meditations. But the early days of loss are a time of spiritual emergency. There will be urgent things that will need your attention: logistical, emotional, both, or more. Your questions will wait, and you may ponder them for years. In the immediate aftermath of the loss, the goal is to simply get through the moments.

A Prayer for You on the Day of Your Loss

Whether in a hospital room, alone on the phone, or in the moment someone turns and walks away, you are not alone.

Whether your tears fall today, a month, or a year or more from now, you are not alone.

May the rain meet the tears when they come; may the sun hold your heart.

May the wind clear the hardest thoughts; may the earth hold you firm.

May your footsteps remind you that you walk the path of every living person who has loved and lost and wept and walked again.

May you remember that in your most empty moments, you are not alone.

The world is with you.

A Ritual on the Day of Your Loss
(Or on Any of the Days Afterward)

You may struggle to connect with your spirituality immediately after your loss. Then again, your connection with your spirituality may feel as though you're on fire, pulsing with power and understanding. Maybe you're somewhere in the middle. The following ritual is designed for you to edit it to suit your needs depending on your current feelings about magick and Spirit. Aside from fire-safety measures, this is a guideline and not a prescription.

Ritual items:
- Paper and pen
- Candle (flame or battery operated)
- Cup of tea, hot cocoa, or whatever is comforting. Don't hesitate to ask a loved one to prepare the drink for you!

Write your name on the paper. It may be tempting to write the name of the person or thing you've lost, but don't. Write only your name, as this ritual is only about you.

Set the candle on top of the piece of paper with your name on it. (If using a flame candle, place the candle in a flame-proof vessel before setting it on the paper.) Before lighting the candle, speak to it the following: "May this warmth hold me in these first days."

Light the candle, or turn it on if using a battery candle.

Drink your comforting drink. Don't give yourself any tasks, such as focusing on manifestation, healing, letting go, or moving on. Now is not the time for "work." Simply allow the candle and drink to create a comfortable space for you.

After taking the time to nurture yourself, you may wish to offer a prayer for who or what you've lost. It's also perfectly acceptable if you don't wish to do so now and only want to focus on yourself.

If using a flame candle, extinguish it when you're ready to close the ritual. You can relight the candle whenever you need to return to this space of comfort. I personally like using battery-operated candles for this work, as I can leave them on for days at a time, keeping that comfortable space going during my toughest days.

If there is any task that you take from this work, it is to be intentionally easy on yourself in the first days after your loss. Just as you'd be gentle (I would hope!) with your body after a physical injury, be gentle with your heart and mind in these tender first days.

Again, the goal of this working is not to banish your grief or turn pain into positivity. The goal is simply to provide a comfortable space for you while you begin your grieving journey. And, my friend, it will be a journey. Let's prepare you well.

2

Navigating the First Days

The early days after a loss are blurry and surprising. Many people find themselves crying, whether a little or a lot. Some feel many things but don't cry at all. Others simply don't feel anything. Grieving people may also find themselves manically cleaning or organizing their homes, or streaming hours of trash television. Some perform all the above, while other grieving people carry on as though nothing happened. These are just a sprinkle of common ways to grieve.

Grief carves paths to our hearts, and each loss carves its own route at its own pace. Sometimes, grief is extremely efficient. When I lost my last relationship, my wide-open heart absorbed the grief immediately, leaving me face down on a friend's living room floor, wailing in rage and despair. The grief over my child carved a route even faster. Aided by hormones, pain, medication, and fatigue, grief pummeled through my heart with a speed and strength reminiscent of the subway I used to ride to work. But other grief I've experienced has kneaded its way in slowly, even sneakily. In high school, I lost two friends in a car accident. Stunned and confused, I didn't cry at the news. I also didn't cry much at their funerals or at the talking sessions our well-meaning teachers imposed on me and my classmates. But a week after their deaths, when I had a sudden urge to look through my yearbooks but couldn't find them, I wailed.

Grief is weird.

It is also full of surprises. It's perhaps expected that grief brings sadness and rage. Grieving people may be surprised at how deep the pain can go, expecting to find a floor beneath the sorrow, but only finding more sorrow beneath it. Another common surprise to many is how the world changes after a loss. Part of the grieving process includes learning to navigate the world after the loss.

Navigating This New World

After your loss, you may be surprised or even disturbed by how the world looks much as it did before. Dishes unwashed before your loss remain undone. Yesterday's pants may still be on the floor. Birds still sing, the neighbor gets the mail, the garbage gets collected. New shows and movies are released, and social media content is shared. People talk about things that have nothing to do with your loss.

Yet, the world has changed. It's your life. But it's not.

It's as though you've been unwittingly moved to an impeccably detailed movie set based on your life, exactly modeling your home, place of work, neighborhood, etc. To the outside eye, everything looks the same. Even to your own eyes, your world *looks* the same. But you know it's not. Perhaps you're like me and you want to shout at everyone passing by, "Hey, assholes! Don't you know the world is completely different? How do you not notice that nothing is the same?"

But the truth is that the world *is* the same. It's we, the grieving people, who are changed. Amid our grieving, we must learn to navigate this identical, but foreign, world.

In the fragile days immediately after losing our child, I watched condolences arrive in my phone via text. I appreciated them but rarely responded. I couldn't remember how to type a reply. Family and colleagues sent meals and flowers, but the food had no taste and I, normally a flower fiend, couldn't remember how to care for cut blossoms. I looked at books I'd always loved, but suddenly couldn't remember what I'd liked about them. I tried wearing my favorite clothes but didn't know why I ever favored them. Even frying an egg felt hard. Everything looked and felt hollow, a shell of nothing. Nothing felt more like a shell than my altar, which immediately began collecting dust.

When I'd pass my altar, I sometimes had flashbacks to finding my old toys in my parents' attic. When I'd look over these toys, I remembered when the dolls, Barbies, and stuffed bears were full of spirits. Like so many children, I firmly believed my toys were conscious. When handling them as an adult, I didn't recognize this consciousness, but they still carried a sweetness and nostalgia. I still loved the toys, even if I no longer believed they could see and hear me. My altar, on the other hand, with its careful collection of once-sacred objects, was suddenly as hollow as the old toys. But instead of inducing that same warm nostalgia, I had a gap in me where anger and feeling betrayed would have fit, if I had those feelings. It's difficult to feel angry at or betrayed by something you no longer believe in. Losing belief in my toys' consciousnesses had taken years, but losing my belief in Witchcraft took only one terrible night.

It wasn't the first time loss made me relearn my world, but it was the first time that I did not have Witchcraft as my guide.

One morning during my senior year of high school, my class was pulled into the choir room. A handful of grim-faced teachers and an unfamiliar priest told us that two of our classmates, whom I'll call Vanessa and Robert, died in a car accident on their way to school. That loss sent me to tarot, crystals, and combing every book on spirit communication at the local New Age store. I wanted to connect with my lost classmates, but more than that, I wanted to know *what* had happened to them. I wanted proof of the heaven my Catholic upbringing had promised, and if they weren't in heaven, where might they be? They were too good of people to warrant hell, and I wasn't sure I believed in hell anyway. If heaven was a myth, then what else was out there? I wanted to make sense of their deaths as I navigated a cold and hard new world where death was real and not some abstract thing worried parents warned us about. Witchcraft helped me grieve that loss.

Years later, when my last relationship failed and I navigated a world where someone I'd loved deeply could be the source of so much hurt, my then-coven was confused and alarmed. They wanted to help me, but they also wanted an explanation. They saw the magick I'd performed to save that relationship. Despite that magick, if I, their leader, could have her heart so spectacularly broken, what did it say for their own magick? Had magick failed me, or had I failed magick? One coven member asked me what I thought the goddess Brigid might be trying to teach me.

"I think she's throwing me down a sharp, pebble-littered path to protect me from some cliff I didn't see," I said. "But I'm still on the mountain, and I can't see that cliff. I don't know how hard I would have fallen."

I navigated the grief of the heartbreak by firmly believing that Brigid had a plan for me and that my magick would ultimately work, bringing me the love I longed for. When I later met my husband, that story made sense. My magick led me away from a person I wasn't meant to be with and to my true love. Belief in that loss's purpose helped me navigate its inevitable grief.

I had no stories to rest against when we lost our child. I couldn't even be angry at Witchcraft. I no longer believed in it enough to be angry. My new post-loss world included a crisis of faith.

Loss During Loss

In my Catholic school education, our religion teachers spoke about losing faith as though it were a problem to solve: Did we ever question our faith? If so, when? Why? How fast could we begin to believe in the Christian God again? We scribbled our answers in notebooks, which we dutifully turned in for feedback and grading. According to our lessons, faith was essential, and if we lost faith, we needed to find it immediately. Inability to resurrect our faith (pardon the pun) was a failure.

Witches often avoid the word *faith*. Perhaps it resonates too much with the religions many of us left behind. We more often use *belief*. We also use *trust*, as in "trusting the magick," "trusting the gods," or "trusting ourselves." But faith, belief, and trust are siblings with only slight differences. One difference is that trust can be broken, and when it is, it's difficult or impossible to repair. Trust exists, or it doesn't. Belief, on the other hand, is malleable. It shifts in different experiences and contexts. Sometimes, belief can be strong enough that we feel we are on fire. Other times, we wonder if we ever believed in anything at all. Meanwhile, faith can be described as choosing to believe in something when there are plenty of good reasons not to, or trusting when there is no evidence that the trust is warranted. One commonality between trust, belief, and faith is that they are rooted in conscious choice.

None of them just happen. None offer a guaranteed reward. We choose to trust, believe, or have faith.

When we grieve, we may question if what we once believed was ever real. We may even start to chalk up our most extraordinary spiritual experiences to imagination or hallucinations. Mainstream religions may openly discuss the experience of having a crisis of faith, but while Witches aren't immune to doubting their beliefs, we rarely discuss our doubting times. Few things shake faith, belief, and trust in one's spirituality more than grief.

In the early days of navigating our new post-loss world, personal spiritual beliefs can be difficult to lean on. Yet, grieving people are often encouraged to "trust," believe," or "have faith" in magick, spirits, gods, or the "will of the universe." Unfortunately, this well-meaning advice is like telling someone who has just broken both legs to simply get up and walk. A grieving Witch may not only feel their loss but also the loss of the spirituality that previously supported them. They may even feel like they're failing at being a Witch.

Alternatively, grief can incite a powerful flavor of belief. Some grieving Witches describe an even greater connection with their spirits, gods, magick, or otherwise. It may be so strong that they wonder if they are losing touch with reality. These feelings, too, can be a natural reaction to loss. In time, these powerful feelings are likely to settle down, possibly leaving the grieving Witch to wonder if they chased away the powerful Magick. If this is your experience, know that you didn't chase anything away or do anything wrong. A heightened sense of the spiritual world following a loss is yet another natural reaction to grief and is often temporary.

Whether a spiked increase or a marked absence, trust, belief, and faith are practices, not end products. Sometimes our faith will consume us. Other times, we'll lack belief in anything. At another point in the journey, our faith and beliefs will be so strong we'll wonder how we ever *didn't* believe. Faith is fluid. Beliefs ebb and flow. Trust is a choice, not a guarantee. A change in our faith, trust, and beliefs is especially normal following a loss.

Remember, if you struggle to believe in magick after your loss, you are not failing as a person or as a Witch. You are simply experiencing the very human reality of losing faith amid grief. On the other hand, if you feel like your magick has become so powerful and your beliefs so strong that you struggle to recognize yourself, there is no need to rush to shape these new beliefs into a new practice. Be patient with yourself. Accept your post-loss beliefs, whatever they may be, for what they are now. You are grieving. You do not need more work to do, whether that work involves reviving old beliefs or tempering strange new ones. Fiery new beliefs will simmer down, and faith and belief are likely to return.

Navigating the Lack of Control

Witchcraft is largely rooted in a belief that it is possible to exert control over our existence. If a spell doesn't go as planned, Witches often reflect on what went wrong in their formula and explore what else can be done magickally to ensure future success. If Witches hit a general spate of bad luck (a sick pet, a rent increase, a lover ghosting, an argument at their job, or a layoff), one of the first things they may do is cleanse themselves or their space of negativity or seek divination to determine if a curse is present. These rituals are meant to regain power over circumstance.

But loss teaches us that full control is an illusion. If someone dies or stops loving us, or the house burns down, no candles, spells, or incantations will resurrect the person, restore the lost love in full, or rebuild the house. Now, many Witches would argue that some magick would bring in new love, or invite the departed spirit to reincarnate in a new form close to the grieving person, or bring along a new house, and this may very well be true for many. However, a newly grieving person doesn't want a new partner, a new home, or their deceased beloved to "return" in new form. They want what they lost in its original form, but no magick will ever provide that. This is one of the hard truths many Witches experience in their post-loss world. We do not have the control we thought we had. This is a humbling, even horrifying, realization.

The good news: A lack of control isn't bad news.

Accepting a certain lack of control eases the pain of the grieving process. When we're not occupied with attempting to control things, we reduce our self-imposed responsibilities. Metaphorically speaking, we stop attempting the impossible task of pushing down a brick wall with our bare hands, and instead give ourselves the opportunity to sit and rest against it. Surrendering control over our circumstances gives us more space to settle into the new world created by loss and let grief be its uncouth, uncontrolled self.

This is one of my many wishes for you, my grieving friend: accept the lack of control. Let your grief be wild. Remember that living with wild grief is hard work. Given that what is lost is most likely never to be found again, take the task of trying to control the uncontrollable off your full, hurting plate.

How Do We Navigate the World Post-Loss?

One of the first gifts I gave myself after my loss was acknowledging that although the world was the same, I was different. The days were long. Individual moments were longer. Nights were eternal. I neglected to respond to emails, forgot appointments, left dishes undone and laundry unfolded. It wasn't that I didn't want to do these things. I honestly did not have the mental focus to do them.

When I sat at my computer, my email account open to reply to a message, I often couldn't remember who I was writing to and why. I might sit and stare at a pile of laundry, as the thought of rolling socks and folding shirts felt exhausting. And I scolded myself for failing at such simple tasks. It was an unfair scolding.

If this sounds familiar, be kinder to yourself than I was to myself. Remember that you are essentially learning how to live in a new world. The routine things you once did without thought (e.g., preparing meals, housekeeping, bathing, caring for pets) will take as much time and effort as though you are learning to do them for the first time. Sometimes, even breathing feels hard. This is normal. You are in a new world. It looks like your old world, but you still need time to learn how to function in it.

Unfortunately, the world does not slow down for grieving people. Some of us are lucky enough to pause our regular obligations while we get our bearings. We may be able to take time off work. We may have help caring for children, pets, or elders. But this isn't possible for all, and many obligations can't wait. You might be able to put off responding to an email, but dependent people and pets still need care, and bills must be paid. Plus, not all grief receives the same level of support. Few, if any, companies allow for their employees to take paid time off after the death of a pet, the ending of a platonic friendship, or a difficult breakup, even though that grief is as real and often needs as much bereavement time as the death of a relative. I am loath to think of the people I pass on the street each day who are forced to carry on with their standard obligations while carrying the unfathomable pain of loss. Whatever freedom is afforded to you, whether it's a generous sabbatical from work or simply a moment to yourself in the bathroom, take it. And breathe.

There will be moments when the grief feels like it will control you forever, but those moments will pass. Some moments will feel longer than others. They will pass too. Not every moment of grief will leave you in tears. Grief manifests in rage, exhaustion, confusion, or even laughter. When a beloved member of my Witchcraft community died and I flew home to be at his memorial service, I laughed when I texted my friends that I was "The Drunk Lady Crying at the Airport," as I'd chosen to try to comfort myself with a little too much wine. We all laughed at the familiar stereotype of a drunk-and-crying airport lady and how that day, that was me. Our collective laughter was a blessing amid the awful loss.

Give yourself the grace of remembering that you have been injured every bit as much as if you had been in a physical accident. You aren't going to move with your regular speed, literally or figuratively.

Allow yourself to move as slowly as your life allows you.

Allow yourself to stop when possible.

Allow yourself to cry when you can.

Allow yourself to respond in ways that may seem odd to yourself or others, such as laughing more than usual or even feeling nothing.

Avoid over-isolating. Even if you are someone who prefers to grieve privately, let a trusted person know what's going on. Let them know if you want space, but at least inform them of your situation. Human beings are not solitary creatures. We are pack animals, and even if we as individuals crave a little space, others should be aware of what we are going through.

Speak to what you need if you know what you need. It's okay if you don't know. After we lost our child, people asked me what I needed, and I would often say, "I don't know." In truth, the only thing I wanted was for our child to still be alive. I wanted the loss to have never happened, and I wanted an explanation for why it did. The things I wanted were impossible. Finally, I thought of one thing I needed: I needed to stop repeating the story. I asked friends for their help by letting others know what had happened in order to avoid pregnancy questions or baby gifts. I also realized what I *didn't* want. I didn't want to be comforted because I wanted the space to cry. I didn't want to hear miraculous stories of people who had children after a miscarriage, as I only wanted the child I'd lost. Sometimes, I needed my husband to sit beside me because I wanted to weep onto his lap. I learned to ask him specifically for that, and I also learned to tell him that sometimes I didn't need his lap. Sometimes, I was okay to cry on my own, which gave him space to attend to his own needs.

Your First Spells or Rituals after a Loss

Although many people may find it difficult to connect to their spirituality in the wake of loss, others will immediately turn to their Witchcraft practice to support their grieving process. While this wasn't my experience when I lost my child, during other grief journeys, my altar was a wonderful place to sit and cry or scream and rage. If you feel called to practice Witchcraft while you grieve, give yourself permission to keep it as simple as you need it to be. Then again, if you're someone who thrives on creating complicated rituals, and if that feels comforting, go for it! Make those rituals as big and grand as you need them to be. But know that you do not *have* to perform complicated rituals. If you only have energy to sit at your altar and light a candle, do it. If you don't even have the energy to light a candle and just want to cry to or rage at your spirits, your gods, or whatever you believe in, great. A beautiful and simple Witchcraft grieving practice includes placing an effigy of what you've lost on the altar to serve as a focus point while you grieve. This can be a photo of the person who passed or a trinket that belonged to them. If this is a relationship, a community, or a physical place you are grieving, the piece might be an object that your former love gave to you, a symbol of the community, or a map of the place you left.

If you are looking for words to say, here is an incantation you can try:

> *Salt of my tears, now flow free,*
> *Spirits of my knowing, be beside me.*
> *I am wounded, I am weak.*
> *Hold me now, in my grief.*

Now, talk to your altar. Tell it what has happened. Tell it what you need.

Maybe sitting at your altar doesn't feel good right now. Altar work isn't necessary if you'd prefer to avoid your altar during this chapter of your grieving journey. Maybe you don't use an altar in your magick at all. Maybe you just want to do something different. No matter what, do feel free to perform this working in a different space if that feels better. When we lost our child, my altar was the last place I wanted to be, but the bath was a comforting, magickal space. If you have a bathtub, consider drawing a bath, sitting in the water, and allowing the tears to fall. It was helpful to me to have a playlist of songs that typically make me cry. Each time I did this ritual, I listened to it until the tears fell, which would happen at different songs on different days. Sometimes, I didn't cry at all, but the practice helped me relax, which gave me more energy to navigate the other parts of the day. If this work sounds appealing to you but you do not have a bathtub, consider making use of the shower. Consider turning off the lights and showering in the dark, using a different soap, or showering at a different time than you normally would (e.g., if you are someone who showers in the morning, try showering at night). Creating some kind of difference in your typical bathing environment will invite your mind to open to releasing grief.

Releasing grief isn't trying to "get rid" of it. Grief is a natural reaction, not a problem to solve. It's uncomfortable, and sometimes we want it to go away, but wishing it away doesn't make it leave. Grief must flow. Giving ourselves a space specifically designed for the flow of grief can help ease an excruciating process.

While it would be wonderful to dedicate hours or days to our grief, this practice doesn't need enormous swaths of time. Carving out even ten minutes in a nurturing space can be greatly beneficial as you navigate your new life on this side of loss.

A Ritual for Adding a New Ancestor to the Altar

Many Witches tend altars dedicated to their ancestors, whether of blood or choice. These spaces are meant to honor and commemorate people or pets who are no longer alive. Some ancestors may be people the Witch knew in life or knew of through stories and pictures. Ancestors can be related to the Witch by blood, marriage, or another association. Ancestors might be people the Witch never met but who inspired their creative work or life, such as artists, movement makers, great minds in their field, or people they simply admire. Quite often, ancestors are deceased friends of the Witch.

The process of adding someone to an ancestor altar can be a painful one, especially if the person was young, the death was sudden or unexpected, or there wasn't the chance to say a proper goodbye. During the height of the pandemic, many people were unable to attend funerals due to COVID restrictions. While this measure prevented further death and injury, the downside was that it denied many the opportunity to ritually grieve in community. In these circumstances, ancestor altars were a great blessing. Adding a loved one to an ancestor altar is its own rite of bidding them farewell, and served many as a healing substitute when it wasn't possible to gather with others. Many Witches find it healing to place a new person on their ancestor altar soon after the loss, while others need more time. Many Witches wait until Halloween (for some, this may also be Samhain or Día de los Muertos) before adding a new person to their ancestor altar. There is no perfect time to do this work. It all depends on what your heart needs.

If you would like to perform a ritual for your ancestors to welcome a new person to the altar, here is a suggested ritual:

Light a candle (many Witches use white candles on their ancestor altars, but the choice is yours). Near the candle, place a picture of your recently deceased beloved or a trinket that either belonged to them or that reminds you of them.

Offer a prayer to your ancestors. If you do not have one in mind, here is one you can use:

> *Beloved ones beyond the veil,*
> *Welcome [name] to your ranks as well.*
> *Let them feast on the gifts of the eternal world.*
> *They share this space now, behold.*
> *May it be so.*

Sit with the candle while it burns. If it is a small candle, such as a tea light, you may be able to sit with it until it burns away. If it's a larger candle, you will want to extinguish it before leaving the altar. (Remember: do not leave your burning candles unattended.) Return regularly and light the candle again, sitting with it and praying for your recently departed. Whenever the candle is finally burned down to the bottom, extinguish it one last time and remove its remnants from the altar.

This is a good time to express your grief to your previously departed ancestors. When I have lost someone, I have often prayed to my ancestors to help guide and comfort the person I've lost as they transition into whatever comes next. I've also asked my ancestors to guide and comfort me. As they once lived human lives, ancestors understand loss. Let these ancestors comfort you and show you the way to navigate your new world on the other side of the loss.

These prayers are best done in your own words, but if you struggle to find those words, here is another prayer you can offer:

> *My loved ones, whom I cannot see,*
> *I ask you now, do you see me?*
> *Hold my tears, my fears, my sorrow.*
> *Walk with me gently as I weep tomorrow.*
> *For all the days I cry for pain,*
> *Let my loss not be in vain.*

Try to make regular offerings to your ancestors, such as leaving out a cup of coffee, tea, juice, flowers, or other things that are beautiful in their honor. Change food offerings daily. I typically put a cup of coffee on my ancestor altar once a week, but when I am deep in grief, I do it more often. This process keeps me in the routine of connecting with them regularly.

One note: It's considered poor practice to place photos of living persons on your ancestor altar. If you or another living person are in a picture with your departed beloved, be sure to cut the image of the living person or people out of the picture before placing it on the altar. If you are grieving the loss of a relationship with a living person, such as mourning the end of a friendship or relationship, do not put a picture of this person on the ancestor altar. But if you would like to commemorate the end of the relationship or simply ask for comfort from your ancestors, consider writing a letter to your ancestors detailing what happened. The letter can then either be placed on the altar or burned. (Be sure to place the letter in a fireproof vessel before burning, and do not leave it burning unattended.) If you burn the letter, tell the smoke to deliver the message to your ancestors. If you'd like, you can place the letter's ashes on your ancestor altar. If this feels all too complicated, simply tell your ancestors what happened by speaking the story aloud.

Keep your eyes open for the help the ancestors send your way. They will.

A Practice for Navigating Grief

Grief is wild. Sometimes it tells hard truths. Often, it lies. One of the big lies it tells us is that we are alone in our grief. We believe we are the only ones who have ever experienced loss. While no two losses are the same, loss is far from unique in the human experience. Possibly more than falling in love, loss is a great unifier among us all. This is a good time to talk to loved ones about their losses and ask them how they navigated their grief, but if you aren't in a mood to hear others' stories, here is a suggested practice for navigating your place in your grief without the input of others.

Find a place outside. Practice safety—do not go to wild, isolated areas alone or public parks alone at night. It does not diminish the practice if you bring along a friend while you do the work. If you do this work at night, look for the moon. Even if it's hiding behind the clouds, know it is there. If it's the day, sit in the sun. Even if the sun is covered by the clouds, it's still there. Don't look directly at the sun (even with sunglasses on), as it could damage your eyes. Just feel it on your skin.)

Reflect on this reality: For as long as there have been people, people have lost. Over one hundred billion human beings have lived on this planet. Each of them existed beneath the same sun and moon that now dance above you. Each of these humans lost something. Some losses might not seem as deep or profound as yours. Some might be even greater. It doesn't matter. The size and scale of the loss means nothing. Rather than separating you from others, your loss has unified you with them. It is one of the precious human experiences you share with every other person who has ever lived: birth, breath, the sun and moon, and now loss. Your experience of loss is one of the things that makes you human.

Recognize. Acknowledge. Acknowledge the presence and reality of loss for the one hundred billion people before you and all those yet to come.

A Blessing for You in the Early Days of Your Grief

May these days touch you gently,
May your wounds be tended with soft hands.
As the tears fall, may they fall freely,
Without judgment,
Without limits.
May they fall cleanly and leave you room to breathe.
May you remember you are one of many,
A blade of grass in a sea of green,
Not anonymous and not unseen,
But one of many, sharing in the breath and beat,
Of what it means to be alive.
Paying the cost of presence in this world,
Through what we have lost,
May you cry and may it be healing,
And may you find a soft place to lay.

Witchcraft and Loss in the Dark of Night

For me, Witchcraft is a craft and an art. It's what Witches do, not what they believe. Witchcraft is about doing the work, and sometimes that's the work of being in our grief, of feeling all the torn, broken places in ourselves. When we experience the loss of a loved one, we can have these tatters and shards of connection with the person we lost that are left kind of flapping in the breeze, leaking fluids. We don't dodge it; we experience it, and over time, we transmute that pain into something positive. I don't want to *not* hurt when someone I love dies. For me, being a Witch and working with grief is owning, naming, and claiming it. When a dear friend of mine died, I sat vigil with her all night. I was in her house, listening to her breathe her last breaths. In the days that followed, some people wanted to hear about that, to rub up against my experience with her, of having been there when our friend died. I think there was a kind of romance to it for them, but there was no romance to it. It wasn't all "sitting around communing with my friend in the oneness of the goddess as she transitions from this world to the next." It was about sitting with a very old, very sick woman as she lay dying. But that's what Witchcraft is about. It's not about knot work, pentacles, and flowery liturgies, who's got the prettiest athame, or "my lineage is more valid than yours because I'm fewer jumps away from some old, dead white dude." Witchcraft is about what you do in the dead of night when your heart is bleeding out because that connection to someone that you love is broken—not severed, but broken. Torn. It's about learning to wrap up those torn places until they've healed over and finding a way of moving forward and still being in relationship with that person: with their memory, with their spirit.

~**Tamsin Davis-Langley (Misha Magdelene***)*

3
The Grief Spiral

A few weeks after our loss, I took the money I'd saved for a crib and went to a writer's retreat on Whidbey Island, Washington, seeking comfort among the trees. Through strange coincidence, many of the other retreat attendees had recently left a church that belonged to a particularly caustic tradition of evangelical Christianity. In learning this, I kept quiet about my Witchcraft. I didn't fear judgment, but rather worried that they might look to me for guidance. My experience as a priestess has taught me that people leaving their religions of origin are often curious about Witchcraft, but I was in no place to guide anyone. However, I couldn't do the writing work honestly without alluding to my experiences as a Witch. During a small-group sharing, one woman's eyes lit up when she figured out I was a Witch. She was one of the former evangelical attendees, and I recognized in her eager, hopeful face the longing to connect with a new path—one of feminine and omni-gendered divinity, free of the rules, judgments, and contradictions that had hurt her. I also recognized myself in her, as I remembered when I longed for a guide on the new path.

I could not be that for her.

"Don't look to me," I replied when she tried to talk to me about Witchcraft. "Witches get lost too."

Not long before, I would have jumped to guide this hungry, lost soul. But at that time, I could only help myself, and that wasn't going very well.

I felt sorrow for myself and for that lost soul. I felt anger that circumstance had put me where others might look to me when I had nothing to offer. I felt shame for not being the guide I wanted to be. And then sorrow again, followed by anger, followed by shame.

I spiraled inward.

Grief: A Natural Spiral

Grief is natural to mammals. When mammals are hungry, they need to eat. When they are tired, they need rest. When they lose, they must grieve. In 2018, a horrified world watched the orca Tahlequah carry her dead calf for weeks after its death. The other orcas in Tahlequah's pod even took turns carrying the calf, allowing the grieving mother a chance to rest.[2] Elephants have been observed in their own grief rituals, gathering in groups and placing branches and clumps of grass over their dead, vocalizing in various ways. When our family dog died, our newer puppy grieved for her, suddenly uninterested in play and putting himself to bed early. For a long time, I had two cats who

---

2. Lynda V. Mapes. "'I Am Sobbing': Mother Orca Still Carrying Her Dead Calf—16 Days Later," *The Seattle Times*, updated May 13, 2019, https://www.seattletimes.com/seattle-news/environment/i-am-sobbing-mother-orca-still-carrying-her-dead-calf-16-days-later/.

never got along. But when one cat died, the other searched for her and slept longer than usual. When she was awake, she constantly sought cuddles and cried when I would move her from my lap. Grief is part of the mammalian experience, and for many species of mammals, so are rites of processing and demonstrating grief.

Yet somehow, we *Homo sapiens* in the West have largely lost touch with grief rituals and possibly even grief itself. Grief seems to confuse people, and certainly frightens many of us. When loss happens to someone we love, we often try to help them "move past it." Grief is quickly labeled, categorized, broken down, and intellectualized. In more recent years, we've been bombarded with memes and social media content that encourage us to "not cry because it's over, smile because it happened," or similar sentiments. But without proper space to grieve, grief doesn't fade. It transforms, rooting into different, deeper parts of ourselves and wearing the masks of anger, depression, "workaholism," other addictions, sabotaging relationships, and more.

When my friends Vanessa and Robert died, our Catholic school hosted a heartfelt service, brought in priests, and gave us an afternoon off from class to talk about our loss with counselors. But none of that prepared us for seeing Robert's father fall to his knees and wail over his son's coffin in the cemetery. It was a grief most of us, teenagers and adults, hadn't seen before, and no one knew what to do with it. It was never discussed except in whispers between us classmates in the halls.

In the weeks that followed, the teachers and administrators offered us prayers, songs, and promises that God had taken our friends to a better place ... but then, without warning, tore down the memorial we built at our deceased friends' adjoining lockers. The principal said it was because "we needed to move on," but we were all aware of an upcoming open house event and how the presence of such a memorial "might deter potential students." Teachers and parents alike were furious when they learned that most of the class snuck off to the woods one night to talk about our friends without their watchful eyes. It was not a time to socialize, they lectured us. Our classmates' deaths were not "an excuse to party." After only a week or so, the adults in our lives told us to "move on and focus on school." Months later, our teachers offered a fifty-minute, mandatory, class-wide session with soft music and an overhead projector image that said, "How did Vanessa's and Robert's deaths impact you?" They seemed confused when few of us wanted to talk. They wanted structure to our grief. We needed space and community.

I look back now and see that these frightened and well-meaning, but ultimately ineffective, adults were trying to provide a platform for us to grieve—but one that they could comfortably control. They tried. They failed. Still, their failure wasn't the fault of their characters, but with a culture that wants to streamline and box-check a wild, raw, and unpredictable process. We call it stages: denial, anger, bargaining, depression, acceptance. People often want to walk their grieving loved ones through these stages, checking the boxes, getting the ugly "job" of grieving "done."

These stages aren't real. Grief is not a checklist. If grief has any shape at all, it might be a spiral.

Spiraling in Grief

Denial, anger, bargaining, depression, and acceptance are frequently described as "stages of grief," an ideology coined by Elisabeth Kübler-Ross. Kübler-Ross's stages of grief were originally intended to describe what many experience when diagnosed with a terminal illness. For years, this system of organizing grief was adopted by the general public as a road map for all grief. But Kübler-Ross, particularly in her later years, claimed that her ideas were widely misunderstood: "[These stages] were never meant to help tuck messy emotions into neat packages. The five stages—denial, anger, bargaining, depression, and acceptance—are part of the framework that makes up our learning to live with the one we lost. … But they are not stops on some linear timeline in grief."[3]

While the experiences reflected in these stages are all very real to the process of grieving, calling them *stages* is inaccurate. These experiences don't fall in any specific order. First of all, not every loss will provide every one of those responses, and many losses will provide others. Responses to grief are less like stages and more like points on a spiral. Sometimes, we'll hit these response points in rapid succession. Sometimes, we'll feel several at once. We won't experience one point, move on, and never experience it again. As we grieve, we'll revisit some points several times, as though we're looping around a spiral. And just as spirals expand, an expanse of time may pass for us when we don't experience any of these response points, and we may begin to think our grief is behind us, only to run into an old point again … or a brand new one.

Our grief spirals are extremely personal and unique to each of us. We might experience some of the classic experiences as Kübler-Ross defined them, or we might only experience a few. We might not experience any of those at all. We will surely have response experiences that are unique only to us. We will, however, experience some grief spiral points once and never again, and experience others repeatedly. Common, unique, or all of the above, our response experiences are likely to manifest in surprising ways.

---

3. Pauline Boss, *The Myth of Closure: Ambiguous Loss in a Time of Pandemic and Change* (New York: W. W. Norton & Company, 2022), 98–99.

For me, the "shock stage" of my grief over my friends' deaths manifested in something akin to wonder. I was in awe of the pure simplicity of death. One day, Vanessa sat next to me in world history class. The next day, her chair was empty. One day, Robert's black hat hung on a rack in the hall. The next day, it didn't. That was it. Loss, as it turned out, was terrifyingly simple. Again, I cried little at their funerals. In the years after that, a certain memory of my friends might make me tear up, but I generally spoke of them with a calm, intellectual distance. If I experienced the "despair stage," it arrived on the tenth anniversary of their deaths as I listened to a friend play a song on his guitar at a theater at 2:00 a.m. on a Sunday night/Monday morning. I was supposed to work at 9:00 a.m., but I didn't feel like going home. I was suddenly awash in sorrow over the fact that my friends hadn't lived long enough to stay up too late on a work night and set themselves up for a bad next day at the job. I sat in the mostly empty theater and cried for them more than I ever had before.

If there was an "anger stage" of this loss, it manifested as jealousy when I was deep into my thirties. A colleague's teenaged daughter lost a friend to a tragedy, and my colleague took time off work to be with her instead of attending an important conference with the rest of our team. I was disturbed at how jealous I was of this girl, remembering how many parents did not even attend our friends' funerals, let alone take time off work to be with us in our grief. I thought of how we'd been told to "stop crying" and how often these parents changed the subject when we wanted to talk about Vanessa and Robert. As an adult, I could rationalize that these adults' unfortunate responses were products of them being from a different generation combined with being triggered by the devastating fear of losing a child. Their only coping process was to try to sweep away the situation as quickly as possible. But that rationale did not stop me from quaking in my hotel room when I was an adult myself, enraged that this poor, grieving girl had her father by her side while she grieved her friend … something my friends and I did not have.

If there was any sort of "bargaining," it was not a single stage or point on the spiral but an ever-present companion. Shaken by the cold inevitability of death, I spent much of my young adult life squeezing in as many life experiences as possible. This meant extreme choices and more extreme mistakes made in the name of life being terribly short. Sometimes, life got too big and wild for me, and I cocooned back into myself only to explode again later.

Even now, I still hit some points on my own grief spiral for those losses. Sure, it's been over twenty years, but a certain song, an anniversary, or coming across their permanently young faces in an old photo album finds me hitting shock, despair, anger, and more all over again.

Witches and the Grief Spiral

Many Witches love spirals. Some imagine them in rituals. Others wear them as jewelry. Some Witches dance in spirals. Spirals have magick. Where does a spiral start, and where does it end? When we are grieving, we ask similar things. We likely know where our personal grief spirals started: at the moment we lost. But we may wonder where they will end. It's possible we won't want the grief to end, as our grief may feel like the last piece of connection to what we lost. For many, their grief spirals start with a compact center, where the spiral points surround the bereaved so tightly that anger can't be separated from despair, shock from bargaining, or any other points unique to the individuals. Some points don't have names, the tortuous feelings exiting without a proper label to describe them.

But we will pass through the madness of the compact spiral origin. The points will separate, and we will have a breath between the responses. Yet, around the spiral we will continue. In the early days of your loss, you may even find yourself hitting the same grief spiral points repeatedly throughout the course of a day. Morning may provide a few hours of rage, which may recede for a little while only to bring despair or shock later in the afternoon. In the very early time after a loss, you may hit points on the spiral several times in an hour.

Others may find that their grief journey begins far on the outside of the spiral, feeling few, if any, of the points, and great expanses of time will pass between them, only to experience several at once years later. For some, the spiral is a slow descent, while others may find themselves drawn in quickly.

A spiral is a solid analogy because grief is messy, unpredictable, disorienting, and dizzying. Grief itself feels as though one was thrown into a physical spiral, spinning round and round, colliding with the different responses that loss provides. Grief is not linear. There are no boxes to check or tasks to complete when it comes to grieving. It is a unique process, every bit as unique to you as your loss, and we spin through it rather than progress through "stages."

Space on the Spiral

Time passes. We sleep, we rise, we eat. We find there's more space between the points on the spiral, deeper breaths between the sobs. We move outward; we expand. We'll start to think we've turned the corner in grief, only to come across another point. It may be the same point we've hit before, a point we thought we'd passed. Sometimes we spiral in and then back out again, hitting the same grief points going in as out. Grief, like everything in this world of ours, breathes and recedes.

When we're in the thick of our grief, we may not be able to imagine a life without grieving. But after a series of tear-fueled days, weeks, or months, we will wake and find ourselves going through the whole morning, even through lunch, without shedding a tear. There's relief in those moments. The spiral has given us a bit of space. But even the space is hard, potentially triggering guilt. *How dare we have a moment's peace after what's happened?* If we stop grieving, does that mean we didn't truly love what we lost? Is it final? Sometimes, grief is the last connection to what we lost. Sometimes, it's the receding of grief that may make us feel as though we've lost again for a second, third, or fortieth time, and this needs its own period of mourning.

Witches are not immune to cultural influences that try to suppress grief. Because grief is often seen as a problem to solve, many Witches encourage "focusing on the positive" in every situation, including loss. But not all sadness is "negative," and not all "negative" is harmful. While there is some merit to embracing a positive outlook, grief is not only necessary, but sacred. It should not be expunged quickly in the name of "positivity." The process of grieving is beautiful, but we don't have to love grief to honor its sacred quality.

Witches often utilize magick as a tool to control external circumstances through things like spellcasting, visualization, and connecting with spirits. But when the external cannot be controlled with magick, we may question our power as Witches and the potential of magick in general. Loss is an external circumstance that can punch a hole through our beliefs in our own magickal abilities. As we explored in the last chapter, no spell or ritual can fully restore what was lost. Does this mean that magick is without purpose?

What if magick is not simply the casting of spells or performance of ritual, but the process of sacred change? If a spell is cast, a ritual performed, and results are witnessed, it can be said that the world is changed through magick. But if we only see magick as an engine to bring us what we want or keep us in control of things around us, we've minimized magick's potential. We've also minimized the potential for experiences like grief to provide their own magick. Grief is its own kind of magick. Without any spells or rituals, grief changes the world because it changes *our* world.

Does this mean that grief automatically changes our world, or us, for the better? I suppose that depends on what one believes is "better." Grief might make us appreciate what we have, but it can also embitter us to the existence of living. It's wonderful to appreciate what one has, but it's not wonderful when stubborn appreciation refuses to acknowledge the pain of loss. A so-called embittered view of life is often brandished as "negative," when maybe this "negative perspective" is merely recognizing a reality and mourning a previous mirage. Many people say grief makes us stronger, and maybe it does. But is stronger better? Strength is often revered as a good thing, enabling us to "power through" whatever it is we're supposed to overcome, but an overemphasis on strength can mask injuries that need healing. Grief can also weaken us. Is weakness automatically a detriment? What might be termed *weakness* is often equated with vulnerability, a state that supposedly invites more injury. But so-called weakness could also provide the opportunity for recognizing and honoring one's boundaries and the boundaries of others.

How grief changes us and whether those changes are "good" is subjective to the person experiencing them. Viewing grief as a sacred, magickal spiral may be helpful when (not if … *when*) you find that certain points in your grief process repeat themselves. This doesn't mean you have failed at grieving. If you feel you are unable to move forward in your life because of grief, it may be time to seek the support of a mental health professional. But repetitious moments of grief response are common. Years after your loss, you may be going about your day as usual when a song starts playing at the coffee shop that reminds you of the loss. You might break down in tears and need to leave the shop, or you may pause and reflect while waiting for your mocha. You may even smile. Grief is unpredictable. We may think we've gotten past a point in our spiral, only to have it slap us again years later.

Ultimately, we don't leave the spiral. But in time, the points on the spiral become less disruptive. Greater time passes between them. We may be on the spiral of grief for a specific loss our whole lives, but eventually the grief will not rule every moment. Plus, there are other gifts to find on the grief spiral: Joy. Peace. Clarity. Perspective.

While processing my jealousy of my coworker's daughter after her own friend's death, I experienced a deep, overwhelming pocket of compassion. From my hotel room, I texted condolences to my colleague and stressed how wonderful it was that he turned down our work trip to be with his daughter. I explained how I, too, had lost friends when I was her age and how much I had wanted the support he was demonstrating, and suspected she would always remember him being there in her time of need. This colleague later told me both he and his daughter cried when they read my text—not because it made them sad, but because they felt seen. His daughter felt her terrible experience was validated, and he felt supported in his choice to be with her. It was a surprising gift for us all, and one that I believe can only be found in the journey of grief.

Other points on the grief spiral might come as moments of clarity, manifesting not as rocks to the heart but as lenses to the eyes, helping us see things slightly (or greatly) differently. Another year, precisely on the anniversary of my friends' deaths, I sat at a bar with a guy I was dating. I was experiencing a point of joy and gratitude on my long grief spiral, feeling grateful for living my strange life. I was twenty-six, constantly short on cash, didn't have much of a plan for my career, and my romantic life was a mess. Still, I was *living*. I had a chance at life that was denied to my young friends.

My date, however, was not feeling the same about life that night. He was angry about some career setbacks, and the more he drank, the angrier he became. I listened, but my thinking was shaped by the troubling anniversary. I tried to point out how lucky he was to even have the opportunity to pursue his dreams, but the more I tried to get him to be grateful (which was its own mistake), the angrier he became. The conversation turned ugly, and my date, several Scotches in by then, said hurtful things. Under normal circumstances, I might have left in tears and waited for him to call to apologize. But because of where I was on my grief spiral that night, I saw something different. Since I had this gift of living, I would not waste any more of my time with this person. I broke up with him right then.

He apologized the next day, and in retrospect, I see that he was going through his own grief spiral for an unrelated matter, which was then manifesting as anger at his career. Still, the night was a gift. Until that night, I hadn't seen that it wasn't the right relationship for either one of us. Grief, in its long spiral, opened the door to better things for us both.

The Wheel, the Spiral, and Sacred Grief

The Wheel of Fortune card is one that often confuses my tarot students. In many decks, it's a card of complicated mythology. In the journey of the tarot, the Fool (the central character of the tarot) has chosen to move forward on their journey after briefly pulling back to seek the wisdom of the Hermit. The Wheel often represents the choice to move on when it might be easier to stay hidden from the world. This, too, is certainly a moment in grief. Isolation has a role in grief, gifting ourselves the space to process our loss, freedom from explaining things, release from others' reactions to our loss. But there will come a time, whether by choice or circumstance, when we must step out of our

isolation. We go back to work, walk the dog, help a family member, celebrate a friend's birthday. But just like the turning of a wheel stuck in the mud, these first movements take great effort. Enormous will and strength are required to turn that wheel.

But in the tarot, the Wheel of Fortune has other profound implications. In *Seventy-Eight Degrees of Wisdom*, Rachel Pollack explores the symbolism of this fascinating card. One of the interpretations includes King Arthur having a vision of a powerful king at the top of a wheel, which the goddess Fortuna turns and ultimately crushes the king at the bottom. It is a message for Arthur that no matter how much secular power a person may hold, their fate ultimately rests in God's hands.[4] When misfortune happens and we cannot understand its reasons, we can assume they are indeed part of a greater plan, aka "God's plan," or as many Witches might say, "Part of the will of the universe."[5] There may be times when this idea is comforting to a grieving person, but it's often more comforting to those witnessing the grief than those

---

4. Rachel Pollack, *Seventy-Eight Degrees of Wisdom: A Tarot Journey to Self-Awareness* (Newburyport, MA: Weiser Books, 2020), 83–84.
5. Pollack, *Seventy-Eight Degrees of Wisdom*, 84.

experiencing it. When we are amid grief, the thought that our loss was based in the will of some intelligent being is horrifying. However, it can also be equally horrifying to think of the loss having no real purpose. Which is it? Is our pain part of some cruel design or some cruel twist of bad luck?

In reflecting on the Wheel in tarot, Rachel Pollack argues that the Wheel does not become visible until we step away. She also suggests that the card represents an unknowable aspect of existence, pointing out that the card contains the Hebrew letters of Yod, Heh, Vav, and Heh again: the unpronounceable name of God in the Jewish tradition, rendering God's true name a permanent secret.[6] When we look at this card and its images in the context of grief, we are exploring a potential purpose to our loss as well as the possibility that there is no purpose for it, and also that there may be something in between purposeful and purposeless: a realm and reason we can't conceive of or ever fully understand.

Pollack also points out the creatures depicted in the Wheel card symbolize death and rebirth. One of these creatures includes the snake, which many traditions utilize as a symbol of rebirth through the shedding of its skin and coming out of brumation in the springtime. The sphinx at the top of the card is thought to represent Horus, the son of Osiris, a god who experiences resurrection. These images, Pollack argues, are symbolic of life triumphing over death:[7] "Life is powerful, chaotic, surging with energy. Give way to it and Horus, the god of resurrection, will bring new life out of the chaos. The Wheel turns up as well as down. ... The important thing about changes is the reaction. Do we accept the new situation and adapt to

---

6. Pollack, *Seventy-Eight Degrees of Wisdom*, 87.
7. Pollack, *Seventy-Eight Degrees of Wisdom*, 88–89.

it? Do we use it as an opportunity and find some meaning and value in it?"[8]

If we compare the Wheel to the spiral, we can view the journey of grief in a few ways. We have space to accept that grief has ups and downs. Sometimes we'll feel high and strong, and sometimes we'll feel we are being crushed. We may sometimes see a purpose to the loss, only to experience confusion and bewilderment over it again at another time. There will be moments when we must sit with the fury and distress of our loss's potential lack of purpose. We don't need to fight these changing realities. We can flow with them. One day of calm and clarity does not have to be considered progress, and following it with another day of tears and rage need not be thought of as regression. Grief is not linear. Remember, if it has any shape at all, it's more like a wheel or a spiral. Recognizing this reminds us that even though we will experience peace on our grief journeys, we may experience pain again further down the road. But also, even when we experience pain, we will once again experience peace at another point.

Call it the Wheel. Say it's a spiral. Maybe for you it's both. Maybe it's neither. Either way, it is a process with many moments of repetition. Release the thoughts of stages and avoid treating grief as a problem to solve or accomplishment to complete. Remember that repetitive responses to your grief are simply part of the experience. Love it, hate it, or feel a mix of both or something else altogether. Just know that grief is working its complicated magick on you. You will be changed. How you will be changed is a mystery yet to be revealed.

The grief spiral will eventually get larger until it's part of your sky and earth. This doesn't mean that you will be overshadowed by

---

8. Pollack, *Seventy-Eight Degrees of Wisdom*, 89–90.

grief forever, but rather that your journey along its spiral has transformed you. We don't go back to who we were before our loss, but we can accept our new reality. There will come a time in which you will move with the spiral and won't feel crushed beneath it. You may even find yourself dancing.

Grief Is the Doorway

Witches understand, profoundly, the invisible. I think that informs the questions we ask ourselves and the questions we ask of universal consciousness, our altars, and our ancestors. There's an expansiveness, which can also translate as overwhelm, because it's so much bigger. We Witches connect the dots of experience. We see a leaf spiraling to the earth in a certain way just as we're walking by and understand that there is a message. We ask what the message is underneath that leaf's spiral, and what the message of the wind on our skin is. Grief cannot be linear. No patent responses will do. Because we energy workers, Witches, spellcasters, work with the elementals, the directions, all the things, we look for the greater interconnectedness in everything that happens. That's very different from, say, someone who has a singular road in life in which everything leads to one answer, whether that's believing in whatever religion, in God's will, or giving up your power and freedom to fate or chance. For grieving Witches, I would encourage the letting of the grief, and encourage as much nonresistance to it as possible. We're working in structures where there's no space for grief, and therefore, there's no space for humanity. Grief is a part of being human. Carve out, create, be insistent about prioritizing time to just be with grief, allowing the tears, allowing your body's natural responses. It's the resistance that can create other problems in the body and confusion in the mind. If the grief is not allowed to move, there's no way to get yourself back. Grief is a rite of passage, a divine point of entry. You must go through it to get back to yourself. Don't resist the call to cry. Take the time, and don't put an end date on it. Do not allow anyone else to tell you when you've grieved enough. Be protective of your process. And what does that look like? It doesn't always look like wailing. Sometimes it looks like long walks in meditation, noticing nature. Sometimes it looks like sharing time, if you have community, a community to greet and receive you in ways that you need. That is tantamount because we're flesh, and the flesh must be honored. Practice making the grieving productive, as in moving these fluids out of the body, like the mucus that you're coughing up. It's not elegant at all, but you have to get it out of the body. And with that, we are able to alchemize it into creation. Sometimes, grief is the only doorway to particular parts of ourselves.

~gina Breedlove, Oracle for Grace and Grief Doula

Practices for the Grief Spiral

Draw: Consider drawing spirals on blank paper during a meditation, prayer practice, or a quiet moment to yourself. As you draw the spirals, speak to your grief as though it were a person separate from you. Express your anger, your sadness, your weird moments of joy. Feel free to yell at your grief, bless your grief, or even curse it if that feels good. No matter how you speak to your grief, draw the spirals while you do it. Some may find it cathartic to burn the paper after the work. Others may want to keep it and continue drawing the spirals on it at a different time.

Write: Journal your feelings about your grief without trying to rationalize, explain, or banish them. Don't force yourself to list what you're grateful for if you're not feeling grateful or try to force out deep, painful emotion if you're feeling peaceful. Simply write about where you are in the grief spiral now: how grief currently rests in your body, mind, and heart. Use words or don't. Some of my journaling includes only ellipses or circles on the pages but no words, as some moments in my grief process had no language.

The Wheel of Fortune: Whether or not you read tarot, consider carrying a copy of the Wheel of Fortune card in your wallet. If you don't have a deck or don't want to break up your deck, consider printing out a picture of the Wheel of Fortune or even using its image as your phone wallpaper for a while. Let the image remind you of the changes grief has in store for you, and that no matter how you feel now, it will change.

Recenter: Remember that this is a moment. When you're steeped in your most painful grieving moments, remember that there will be future moments that don't feel so hard. People will say there are brighter days ahead, and yes, that's true, but sometimes those days feel very far away. Practice moment to moment. When the moment is hard, it will pass. Maybe it will take ten minutes, maybe an hour, maybe the rest of the day. But the moment will pass. Another will follow. It will also pass.

Breathe: Breathe not to stop the grief but to disperse it, giving it more space and not letting it all curl up into one place in your body.

Treat tears as a normal bodily process: Just as we need to relieve ourselves of bodily waste, tears need to be released. Take crying breaks whenever you can. I prefer to cry in a place where people aren't going to comfort me to try to stop my tears. I make a lot of use of public bathrooms. I cry a lot in my car. In the earliest days after my loss, tears would sneak up at inconvenient times, and I would need to stop what I was doing to have a cry break. I learned that the more I fought the tears, the harder they were to prevent. When I gave myself crying breaks, I sometimes thought I might never stop crying. But I would. And I would feel better when I did.

Drink water: Grieving makes it hard to remember to take care of our bodies, and dehydration is a great stressor on the body. Bodily stress can needlessly exacerbate grief. Drinking water can make things a little easier. Consider setting reminders to yourself to drink a glass of water, maybe even utilizing timers on your phone. Regular water removes one more stressor while you navigate an already stressful situation.

A Ritual for Your Space on the Spiral

Go to your sacred space, or create one if you don't have one. Bath rituals are particularly helpful if you live with people who are not supportive of your Witchcraft practice. Doing this work outside is a wonderful thing if you have access to natural spaces. Practice safety measures: if you are going by yourself, let someone know where you'll be and bring a phone. Do not put yourself in physical danger for the sake of a Witchcraft practice. If you don't want to be alone or require the assistance of a support person for mobility, don't hesitate to bring someone along.

Consider bringing along the depiction of your spiral, if you created one, and a picture or copy of the Wheel card from a tarot deck, if you have one. If you are in a place where you can burn a candle, consider lighting one. Battery-operated candles are perfectly fine, especially if you cannot use flame in your home or if you live in an area that is vulnerable to fire.

Breathe deeply, focusing on your heart and gut. If you feel pain, where do you feel it? Breathe deeply, allow the breath to touch the painful places. Breathe again. And again. With each breath, ask the pain, "What hurts most today?" If the pain answers, accept it without questioning it, analyzing it, or "shoulding" it into something else.

Speak to the grief. Honor it, bless it, or even curse it. There are no rules on how you speak to grief in this moment.

Finally, ask what you need from the grief: Is it to give you some space? Is it to transform into something else? Is it to just be there?

After your conversation with your grief, if you brought your spiral or a copy of the Wheel tarot card with you, take a moment to look at it. If a revelation comes to you about how the grief is affecting you, honor it or even make notes about it. If nothing comes to you, that's fine. I often find my revelations will come in dreams or synchronistic moments in the days after my ritual workings.

A Blessing on Anger

When the grief turns to rage
The white-hot emotion that wants to devour everything
Curling at the corners and edges of memories,
Uncontained and uncontrolled,
I pray for your grief's direction
I pray for clarity in your anger
A clean and clear path
I pray you have the space to sit with your anger
And courage to look in its face
To recognize its power
Its place
Its wonder
For you are alive
And you are human
And to be alive and to be human is to rue the moment you lost
And rage for what was taken
To give yourself the space to be the toddler you once were
All desire and will and no time or patience for rational
*   thought meant to nail your wild impulses in place*
I pray you have the clean and clear space to turn the rage
*   outward*
That those around you give you the calm and space you need
For your anger not to latch onto the love you still have
To propel you forward
To turn to hard laughter when it's ready
To leave you when you crave freedom from its hot grasp.

4
Moving Through the World after Loss

In a perfect world, we'd all get plenty of time to rest and process our grief before returning to jobs or social obligations. Even those fortunately able to take time to grieve their losses must eventually return to the world. Unfortunately, no griever can return to their lives alone. Grief will come with them, often behaving like a clingy ex-lover. Although you may be ready to let them go, Grief isn't ready to let *you* go.

Perhaps you go to a club or a dinner party hoping to get space from Grief. Grief tags along anyway as an awkward, brooding presence that no one invited, but no one knows how to ask to leave. Even though you made it clear to Grief that they need to give you space, Grief sticks by your side as your default date. It might be awkward for friends and acquaintances. They know Grief is there. They know Grief is quietly giving you trouble. They probably wonder if they should interfere but aren't sure how. They try to keep the conversation light, hoping to keep you from getting pulled into whatever trouble Grief would like to engage you in.

You might drag Grief to the bathroom (aka, drag yourself to the bathroom) and scream at Grief to step aside. That conversation can easily lead to tears, and even if you take the time to fix your mascara, people at the party surely know the fight happened. They might look at you with pity, and that might upset you further. You could try ignoring Grief, but you may find that the more you ignore Grief, the bigger presence Grief becomes. You may realize you're not paying attention to the fun thing you came to do because you're expending your energy ignoring Grief instead. At a certain point, you may realize that everyone else is focused on ignoring Grief too. You wonder if you shouldn't have come at all.

If you're out with people you know well and trust, you can ask for a place at the table for Grief. You'll do your best not to let Grief dominate the conversation, but even you can't control how Grief might behave that night. At some point during the night, someone might say something that irritates Grief. Grief may respond with an awkward or barbed comment or laugh loudly at an inappropriate time. You may get angry with Grief and might drag Grief back to the bathroom where you scream into your fists, shed a few more tears, maybe even text someone who knows and understands Grief. Hopefully, they'll remind you that Grief's behavior is not a reflection of you. The people you're out with will surely understand too. They've likely met Grief before. Still, you may feel like you're the only person who has ever brought Grief to a party.

Maybe one night you're just not able to separate enough from Grief. You might fall into Grief's arms, dancing slow and tight in the corner of the room with Grief, maybe even slipping out the door with Grief when you think no one notices. You might go home with Grief, loathing Grief but also accepting that Grief is not going away. It may be that you'll have to accept that separating from Grief is far more complicated and difficult than you have energy for now.

Perhaps the next day you're ashamed of the way Grief behaved. You may wonder if people felt sorry for you, or if they thought you were rude for sneaking away with Grief. You wonder if anyone will ever invite you out again, or if they think Grief is just a part of you forever.

Fortunately, most people have had their own dalliances with Grief. They've had awkward nights with Grief at their side. If they seem unsympathetic, they may not want to remember.

The First Tender Steps Back into the World While Grieving

Sadly, even if they've had their own losses, people in our lives may not understand the nature of our specific pain. If we lose a pet, we may find people saying, "It was just a dog" or "I'm not really a cat person." If we've lost a romantic relationship, others may say, "I never liked them anyway" or "Let's get you back out there to meet someone new!" And upon the painful ending of a friendship, others may say, "So what? You're better off without them" or simply roll their eyes when we mention our suffering. No matter the loss, grieving people are far too often encouraged to "get back on their feet," to "move on" or "move forward," and essentially get back to "normal" as soon as possible. Even when grieving people might be aware of this and attempt to take the necessary care of themselves, it is hard to escape the pressure to rush healing. Sometimes we may convince ourselves that we've moved on from grief. We may have convinced ourselves that we are ready to face the world again as we always have, only to find ourselves on shaky footing. On my first night out after losing our pregnancy, I thought I was ready to be around people. I wasn't.

Our home, normally comforting, had grown suffocating. I was sick of crying and staring at walls. I was sick of me. It was a cool, clear summer night, and my husband and I made dinner plans with a friend. Our friend is a deeply compassionate soul, and when another group brought a newborn baby into the restaurant, she asked if we'd rather go somewhere else. I thought about it, but declined. Babies are part of life, I reasoned. Plus, I was proud of how unbothered I was by the presence of the baby.

But as the night went on, I drank too much wine. It was the first time I'd had alcohol since before the pregnancy, and it hit me hard. Our friend ate little all night and mentioned being hungry but wouldn't eat more because she was dieting. I don't like diet culture, and a friend going hungry because an app said she'd had enough food would have irritated me even on a good day. But that night, it enraged me. When I woke that morning, I'd looked in the mirror and was at least ten pounds leaner than even a few days prior. Whatever weight my body accumulated to help with the growing baby had vanished with sickening speed. The change was a cold, cruel reminder of what I had lost. Seeing a baby in the restaurant didn't upset me, but a friend willingly putting herself through an ordeal to make the same bodily change that had happened to me under horrific circumstances upset me so much that I snatched her phone from her, tried to delete her diet app, and said something rude about her choice to diet. She left the table in tears, and my husband rightfully pointed out that I was out of line. The next day, I apologized, and luckily, this kind friend accepted my apology.

Grieving people are hard to be around. We take things personally. While the company of others can be refreshing, it is also exhausting. Our fuses are shorter. We may not laugh at a joke, or we might laugh at something that isn't funny to others. Sometimes, just getting out of the house feels strange. Noises are louder. Lights are brighter. Others' happiness can feel like an insult. How dare they be happy? Don't they know what's happened? Time slows down. It also speeds up. Ten minutes crawl by, but then an hour evaporates. You may find yourself forcing reactions to others' stories and jokes, fumbling to remember how to laugh, look impressed or shocked, or even struggle to remember what an appropriate reaction might be. Maybe, like me, you find yourself inadvertently monopolizing conversations, subconsciously increasing the padding between you and your grief: If you're talking, then maybe you're not thinking about what you've lost.

No matter what happens, be gentle with yourself. Be gentle with others too. Sometimes the outside world irritates old grief: the holidays may make you mourn a lost parent or a childhood you never had. Maybe a birthday party reminds you of estranged family members or alienated friends.

Then again, maybe in your grief you feel desperate to hear music, dance, sing karaoke, or walk in the woods. Being out in the world can break up the reel in our heads replaying what we lost and leaves room to find compassionate others. When I was eighteen, I split with my boyfriend in the afternoon and went to my waitressing job that evening, freshly heartbroken. An irritated cook asked why I was forgetting forks and messing up dinner orders. When I explained what had happened, his face softened.

"If it makes you feel better," he said. "I've been there."

It did. My young mind unconsciously believed that I was the only one who had ever had a broken heart. It was comforting to learn that everyone around me had, at some time, experienced loss: The deli guy. The librarian. The people in the cars before, beside, and behind me. Every single person I saw had lost, lost, and lost.

One cruel aspect of the pandemic years was that they robbed us of the mechanism of distraction. Those who craved distraction from whatever grief they experienced were forced to grieve alone during long lockdowns. The pandemic itself was a kind of grieving: grieving the world we once knew. In many ways, that grief continues. It is 2023 as I write this, and while in many (although not all) parts of the world the mask restrictions and lockdowns have lifted, the virus is not gone from the world. Immunocompromised people must still live with the restrictions most of us experienced before. There is also a question of "but will it?" that follows us. We can plan the party, circle, gathering, or conference, but we can no longer count on things as we once did. In some ways, this makes gatherings even more sacred, but there is grief over collective lost stability. For this grief, there is no plan. We must all learn to move through it together.

How Grief Affects Witches out in the World

In some ways, grief makes me a kinder person. When my grief is particularly thick, I consciously treat each person I meet as though they, too, are grieving, intentionally making softer requests and utilizing more patience. You could say this is how we ought to treat each other always, and maybe that's true, but it's easy to forget grief exists when it isn't fresh.

Obviously, given my story above, I do this with *widely* varying degrees of success. There are times when I feel resentful of others if they are not visibly grieving. This resentment stems from an imaginary world where I am the sole griever and everyone else is happy. Of course, it is not only untrue but exacerbates my grief. Grief feels heavier when we believe we are the only ones to ever experience it. I counteract this resentment by embracing the practice above and trying to treat everyone I meet as though they are experiencing the same grief that I am. Not only do I find that it makes my interactions with others easier, but I feel more supported in my grieving process. That support comes from myself. It's not dependent on anyone to offer it to me.

Sometimes, grief is so draining that we don't have the space to be kind. Sad, stressed, or overtired children will throw things or lash out at caregivers. This does not mean they're bad children. They simply have an unaddressed need and are crying for help. Adults are no different, but we lash out in other ways. Grief can make us impatient, quick to anger, unsympathetic to the struggles of others, and more. That doesn't make us bad people, but simply people who have specific needs due to our grief. It's good to acknowledge when our grieving state has caused us to be unkind to others, even if we only acknowledge it privately. Catching ourselves in these moments is *not* an invitation to criticize ourselves, but rather to recognize that our grief may be telling us that we need some specific kinds of care and perhaps a little more space from the outside world.

When those moments come up, ask yourself what you're truly craving: Sleep? Space? A mindless movie or show? When you name it, make getting or doing it a priority.

Don't Skip Caring for Yourself Because "Someone Else Has It Worse"

Yes. Someone out there, maybe on the other side of the world, had a worse breakup, a more traumatic injury, a more devastating betrayal. That's guaranteed. But it doesn't mean you shouldn't be cared for. If you broke your ankle, would you skip medical treatment because someone else broke a leg? Or if you broke your leg, would you delay a trip to the doctor because someone else broke their back? I sure hope not. Ignoring such injuries would only set you up for even more challenges in healing later. Saying, "Why do I have the right to cry? Someone out there has it worse…" is more of an escapist act than a virtuous one. It suppresses your grief into deeper recesses of your heart and soul. It will come back, and when it does, it is likely to cause even more damage to yourself and your relationships. Ignored grief hurts us, our loved ones, and our ability to enjoy life.

You deserve joy. Your grief doesn't deserve to be ignored.

Guarding and Shielding When Grieving

Many Witches have the natural ability to connect with the energies of others. Some refer to this as being empathic. I personally believe it's simply being human. As humans, we are innately in tune with the rhythms and emotions of others of our kind. Some are more sensitive to this than others, but it does exist in all of us. The practice of Witchcraft opens these natural human senses even further. Grief heightens these senses as well, which means that a grieving Witch can be a force of uber-sensitivity. My hope for you, as a grieving Witch, is that you can be extra mindful and supportive of yourself while you grieve—whether that grief is fresh or a resurgence of grief from a long-ago loss.

Grounding and *shielding* are common Witchcraft terms. They are generally used to center and protect oneself when performing magick, whether the Witch believes in negative forces that can interfere with the magick or would simply like an additional ritual to support their focus. Some Witches employ these techniques before entering stressful or antagonistic situations. This work is particularly helpful when grieving. As grief opens our hearts and other senses, it leaves us vulnerable to new hurts or energetic interference (aka, when nasty external energies seem to stick to us). The following section includes an easy grounding practice to explore before engaging with the outside world.

Check In with Yourself

Take a breath. Allow this breath to touch every part of you. Do you feel hurt or constricted anywhere? If so, where? Breathe again onto this place or places. Listen. The pain or discomfort has information. Let it tell you if you need to be out and about now. If the answer is no and you do not *need* to be somewhere, give yourself permission to stay home. If possible, be honest with others. Don't fake illness: tell others that your grief needs support. Be a part of the process to end the stigma and treat grief like the true injury it is.

But as we unfortunately know, we can't always stay home. Jobs or other obligations don't always leave space for grief, or the desire for distraction is greater than the grief itself. If you need to be out and about, here is a simple shielding ritual that may prove helpful.

A Ritual for Shielding Through Grief Acknowledgment

Do the breathing exercise above, taking note of not only where the pain resides but also spaces of pleasure, weakness, strength, or otherwise in your body. Don't judge or analyze it. This is not a time to say to yourself, "I feel tired, but I shouldn't feel tired. I slept all night" or "I feel hungry, but I shouldn't because I just ate." Instead, simply say to yourself, "I feel tired" or "I feel hungry." Simply acknowledge the different feelings in your body, naming each one as you recognize them.

Next, acknowledge the state of your heart. Where is the grief rooted today? Grief may be rooted in resentment as described above: anger at or jealousy of other people who don't appear to be experiencing grief. Grief may also make you laugh at something that would ordinarily seem inappropriate to laugh at. Grief may simply be a ubiquitous blanket of sadness. Wherever grief resides today, name it. Acknowledging grief does not rid us of it, but when grief is ignored, it screams for attention, and often when you need it to be quiet (such as when speaking to a customer or sitting in a staff meeting). If we take a few simple moments to say to grief, "I see you. I hear you. You are not forgotten," grief doesn't push as hard to make itself known. When acknowledged, grief can take a seat and let you do what you need to do.

Take as many opportunities as you can to acknowledge your grief while you are out and about. Slipping away to the bathroom or going for a brief walk around the block can give you the space to do the ritual.

Grounding Your Grief

For me, part of the acknowledgment ritual included cry breaks, a process I strongly recommend if it's available to you. When I first returned to work after my loss, I turned off the camera on plenty of Zoom calls (recognizing that I am quite privileged to have work that allows me to do this) to cry. I also spent a lot of time in bathrooms, both at home or in public places, simply crying. Each time, the tears were so thick and deep that I feared I wouldn't be able to stop, ever. But each time, they did. Sometimes, only two minutes of deep, hard crying would give me remarkable peace for hours. Just as grief is gentler to us when it is acknowledged, tears appear less often when given space to flow.

A Ritual Without Tears

If you're not someone who cries or it's not feasible for you to take cry breaks, it may be helpful to dedicate a few moments to your grief at the start of your day or before leaving the house. Consider trying the following:

Place a beloved crystal on your altar or in your sacred space. If you do not have a crystal or do not typically use crystals, collect any rock from your yard or a nearby park. It doesn't have to be large. If you don't have an altar or a dedicated sacred space, take the crystal or stone to a quiet space in which you feel safe. Beside your bed is a fine place for this work.

If you have the time and space, consider lighting a candle. Any color candle will do, but colors especially good for this rite include blue or purple, as they are peaceful and gentle. Whether or not you use the candle, hold your rock or crystal to your heart and ask it to ground your grief while you are out and about. If you are at a loss for words, here is an incantation you can use:

Crystal, stone, earth's strong bone,
Wait for me, far from home,
Hold my strength, courage, fears,
Until I'm home to release my tears.

Tell your crystal or rock what, if anything, you are nervous about while navigating the world as a grieving person. Describe your worst-case scenario ("I'm afraid I'll start sobbing at dinner and I won't be able to stop…." "I'm afraid I'll scream at a customer and I'll get fired…" "I'm afraid I'll say something rude to someone I love or laugh at an inappropriate time and embarrass myself."). You don't need to plan to address your worst-case scenario, unless formulating a plan is helpful to you. Just acknowledging it will support you.

Leave the stone on your altar, in your sacred space, or in some other safe place and go do what you need to do.

When you return, sit with your crystal or stone again. Thank it for holding space for you. Consider infusing your bath that night with salt, apple cider vinegar, or a combination of beloved herbs that are safe to use in a bath (always research any herbs before using them). If you don't have a bathtub or simply prefer a shower, place these items in a pot of water, soak a washcloth in it, and use it as a scrub in the shower. If your crystal or stone can be submerged in water, consider adding it to the bath. If your stone or crystal cannot be submerged in water, setting it beside the bath or shower is a good alternative. (Always research the solvency of your crystal or stone before dropping it in the bath. Certain rocks or crystals can dissolve or even become toxic in water, so be sure to do your due diligence.)

The goal is to leave the crystal or rock in a specific place in your home, such as on your altar or on a bedside table, to hold sacred support for you while you navigate the world. However, you may feel called to carry the rock or crystal with you, and that is perfectly fine!

If you do decide to carry the crystal or rock with you, I recommend giving it a place and space to rest after your time with it (again, on an altar, bedside table, or other intentional space). Consider performing a smoke cleansing on it if you've been carrying it around a lot, such as burning bay leaves or dried rosemary and wafting the smoke around it.

While it may be disappointing if you lose the crystal or rock, it's not a failure. The wonderful thing about crystals, rocks, or stones is that they are never truly lost. With few exceptions, they do not disintegrate in the elements during our lifetime and will still be part of the earth for as long as you walk on it. It may even be the crystal or rock's intention to leave and take a piece of your suffering with it.

If the crystal or rock vanishes but you feel that you need to continue the ritual, it is fine to get another to put in its place. It may also be that the crystal or rock's disappearance marks a time to do different work for your grief. If you're not sure, take a day off from doing the ritual. If you find yourself struggling much in the same way as before you performed the ritual, go find another rock or crystal and do the work.

Ask for Help When You Need It

Social media has its problems, but it can be a quick and easy way to find additional support. If you have connected with Witches online, a simple post asking for a lit candle or a few prayers can feel good. Let people know if there are things you *don't* want, such as advice, spells, energy, or to answer questions.

If social media doesn't feel good right now (plenty of people withdraw from social media while grieving, as it can be quite draining), consider asking a trusted friend, whether they are a Witch or not, to hold space for you. Ask them to text you an affirmation or adorable pet pictures, perhaps at an appointed time. Giving people a simple, tangible thing to do for you is a great way to gather support. It is also good practice in thinking about what you personally need. Taking time to ask for something small but meaningful helps us be better in tune with what our greater needs are in this process.

You Don't Have to Pretend to Be Okay

Some may find it helpful to pretend to be okay. Fake it 'til you make it, right? There's truth and practicality to that. If you feel better for a brief time by pretending you're not grieving, go for it. However, know that you don't *have* to do that. Let me assure you: you don't have to be okay, and you certainly don't have to pretend to be okay.

If you're feeling particularly not-okay one day and can stay close to home, do it. Eventually, the desire to be around others will return. You are not letting anyone down if you need to take space for yourself. But do yourself a favor, and do our general cultural trajectory a favor, and simply say, "I'm not ready to be around others." It's not only a gift you give yourself, but also one you give others. Someone seeing another take space for their grief helps normalize the process and will make it easier for them to do that for themselves when they need it.

At the same time, do not take it personally if others go forward with their plans and lives while you are taking space. The work or school project, the long-planned trip to the beach, or something else: if you opt out, don't expect others to opt out too. Be supportive of their choice to move forward with their things, particularly if they supported your choice to step back.

Where Are the Gods? What about the Ancestors?

In the months after our pregnancy loss, I didn't attend public Witchcraft events. This was less about my grief and more about logistics. We were still in pandemic lockdown, but even so, I don't imagine I would have felt healed and empowered by public rituals. If I had any belief in the gods or the Craft at all at that time, it was that they were utterly useless to me. Perhaps they were useless to everyone.

But on some mornings, I would wake remembering a day I once spent at an amusement park. The day started pleasant and warm, but the weather turned stormy, and early in the afternoon, the park shut down. While my date and I waited for the bus that would take us home, I watched lightning crack the sky and hit the earth around us. Sitting in that parking lot, vulnerable to the elements, I imagined my most ancient ancestors, thousands of years ago: their vulnerability, fear, and wonder at events such as that thunderstorm. I imagined how they might have developed rituals, prayers, songs, and lamentations to help them navigate frightening, uncertain circumstances. They surely wanted to invoke something to protect themselves from the terrifying reality of being small and human in a giant, violent world.

Sitting there, I offered a prayer to whatever gods might be listening to protect me and my date from the weather, but a chilling and humbling realization followed. Lightning was part of the earth's ecosystem. Lightning needed to happen, and lightning would not intentionally strike me, nor would it try to avoid me. The gods didn't cause the storm, and the gods couldn't prevent it either. What I was witnessing was greater than any god. So, if the gods didn't cause the lightning and they weren't protecting us from it, what purpose did they serve?

Immediately, another thought came to me. Maybe the gods interact with the world in the way that park rangers interact with wildlife. Park rangers observe the environment. They set up protocols to protect the animals within the park from the outside world, but they do not interfere. They don't protect baby bison from wolves. They don't shelter animals from foul weather or feed them when natural food sources become scarce, as that would set the animals up for even more harm. Could it be that the gods are present for us in that way? Would the intervention of a higher power degrade our world in a way we can't imagine?

Maybe.

Maybe there is truth to my realization. Maybe it was only a story I told myself while seeking a moment of comfort. Maybe that's all the gods have ever been: a story to put our fears at ease when everything feels lost. Or maybe they're just watching because letting us navigate these wild landscapes of life is what is best for us.

Either way, the memory of that day helped me stop digging for an explanation as to why the gods had led me into grief. They hadn't. They didn't create my circumstances, and they weren't going to uncreate them. It was up to me to navigate them myself, choosing to trust that something greater, wiser, and more powerful than me may be watching.

Maybe that is enough.

Grieving the Lost Family

I chose to separate from my family of origin because of extreme trauma. I had endured, to put it very broadly, physical, sexual, mental, and emotional abuse growing up. I made the decision around sixteen to seventeen years old that if I wanted to survive, I would have to leave. At first, there was freedom from the fear that I had endured. But I come from a very big, Latine family, and there's a big sense of community. I lost that. A lot of my grief came from not having the big gatherings we would have, cultural celebrations, and things like that.

I'm Indigenous, so I also had to navigate preserving cultural traditions. The grief came from figuring out how to preserve who I am and where I come from, but also bypass the people who hurt me. That was tricky. One of the big ways I navigated this grief was through food. I learned to cook from my father, and despite everything, I was taught a lot about my own culture through cooking a meal and putting good energy in that food. It was healing—a little bit of home but without the trauma.

When I was around eighteen or nineteen, I dove into my Indigenous side, and I started developing a relationship with IxChel—the main goddess of the Maya. She has three forms—Maiden, Mother, and Crone—and she became my mother. Through her and reconnecting with nature, I healed a lot of grief. I've also done a lot of meditation, because deep trauma lingers in and literally changes your body. I make sure my chakras are aligned, working with them individually, and if one goes off-kilter, I smudge everything and do what's called a *limpia*. I clear myself and start at the base level.

In time, I also created my own family. Not just having kids, but having close friends that I consider family. It's about surrounding myself with people that I connect to deeply. When you lose a relationship, the universe is making room for greater things in your life. That is something I'd want others experiencing this kind of grief to know, and that it gets better and clearer. Grief won't weigh you down in the future in the way it does right now. There is a point where you realize you've lost a lot. But instead of focusing on what you've lost, think about what you're about to gain. You have to train yourself to look forward. The grief hits you at different points. You can have a lot of emotions, and there's nothing wrong with being angry or crying. But emotions come in waves, and you'll see that it will hurt less as time goes on. It will occasionally pop up, and that's fine. When it pops up for me, I just acknowledge it and then I cook something. It gives me a little of what I'm missing. I still have who I am. I have my culture with me. I know that I am resilient and I'm going to be okay.

~**Mónica Divane**

5

Grief and Compassion

Compassion is a surprising companion on the grieving journey, and one that we may not realize is there until it gently raises its velvety head. Grief can make us more compassionate to the pain of others, and even more protective of others who are grieving. Compassion also serves as a resource for ourselves when the journey gets difficult. We will need it as we experience the fumbling of others, well-meaning or not, as they try to support or shortcut our grieving journey. But first and foremost, we need it for ourselves.

Grief is exhausting. Whether fresh or being met again long after the loss, grief makes even simple things harder. We forget obligations. We slip on our share of the housework. We forget loved ones' birthdays or special occasions. We're just not as present for the people in our lives. Sometimes, we even hurt them. I learned how a grieving person can harm others not through my own grief journey but through that of a friend.

Years ago, a friend and coven sister experienced two enormous losses within a few months of each other. I had poured myself into our friendship (hello, codependency!), giving all my spare time and mental space to trying to support her. At the same time, I was in a complicated dynamic with an ex. When my grieving friend began dating him, I was livid. How dare she, I thought. After all the care and concern I'd given to her feelings, had she no regard for the fact that I still had feelings for this guy … even though our courtship was technically over? I felt so deeply and personally betrayed that I said cruel things and cut her out of my life, responding harshly whenever she tried to reestablish contact. Other friends tried to help me see her side of the situation, but I refused to hear it.

A couple of years later, I performed a new moon cleansing ritual on myself. I didn't have a specific intention for the ritual, only to release what I didn't need anymore. The ritual consisted of some simple quiet time in the bath with a heaping lump of sea salt in the water. I hadn't even thought of my former friend in quite a while. But the next morning, I gasped when I woke with a stinging realization.

"If a starving person stole food off your plate, would you condemn them?" I swear I heard a voice say, "Would you say they betrayed you, especially if you weren't planning to eat that food?"

Of course not, I knew. I might not like my food being stolen, but I wouldn't condemn a starving person for taking it. My grieving friend was starved for comfort, pleasure, for any shred of joy after so much loss. She found that for a time with my ex. Setting aside for a moment that even calling a former romantic interest "mine" was incorrect (no person belongs to anyone but themselves) and that this former love interest had his own responsibility in this situation, I recognized that while my hurt feelings were valid, my friend was not a selfish person who betrayed me. She was a grieving person filling a need for emotional comfort, one every bit as human as filling a hunger with food. Even though I was within my rights to step away from the friendship and care for myself, she hadn't deserved the cruel words I threw at her.

Before the coffeemaker could finish making the first pot, I emailed her and asked if we could get together, including that I understood if she did not want to see me. She agreed, and when we met, she graciously accepted my apology. Our paths have since taken us in different directions, but the lesson stayed with me. If I could relive that whole situation, I like to think I would have taken a break from the friendship while she explored the relationship, but I wouldn't have been unkind about it. I would have wished her well in doing what she needed to do, and perhaps ask that she grant me the courtesy of giving me the space I needed. I would not have labeled her as a bad friend or shaped the story as one of betrayal. It wasn't betrayal. It was grief.

Hey, You, Go Easy on Yourself

You may pride yourself on being the One Who Fixes Everything, whether in your family, friend group, magickal community, or otherwise. But you are likely to find that you won't have the mental or physical energy to do that while you are grieving. It's okay. You're allowed to let things drop. You may do things that cause you to call yourself a "bad friend." It's okay. There will be time to make it up to people when you've adjusted to your post-loss world. Grief takes up an enormous amount of space in our hearts and minds, making us run like old laptops with too much data on the hard drive. We're going to be slower. We're going to miss the mark.

Repeat after me: "I'm grieving. And it's okay."

When I began Witchcraft, a commonly repeated tenet was "harm none." This idea is largely falling out of favor with modern Witches for many reasons, one being that it's not possible. Harm happens whether we mean to or not. Some harm is necessary for survival. I'm a meat eater, which causes harm to the animals I eat. Even if I were vegan, I would cause harm to the plants I consume. I cause harm to weeds when I pull them from my yard, but most of them are invasive and cause their own harm to native species. I cause harm to the planet when I drive my car, but it's necessary when I want to buy groceries or visit my family. As a Witch, I have cursed and hexed. My choice to curse and hex has been largely rooted in preventing others from causing harm to me, my family, or others. I am personally mindful to not use magick out of jealousy or in response to an ego-bruising. On a non-magickal note, I try not to say hurtful things when I'm angry or tired. However, I'm human and it happens. I've said mean things out of anger or fatigue, and I've cast curses when there was no real threat to me. I've tried to take accountability and correct my errors later. Mistakes happen. It's life.

As a Witch, one code I personally live by is to minimize the harm I cause whenever possible—whether intentional or not—and take responsibility when I do. When we grieve, it may be helpful to remember an idiom often spoken in 12-step programs: "Hurt people hurt people." While we grieve, we may hurt people. Because we may not be able to be fully present for our loved ones, they may feel ignored or abandoned. We may lose our patience because our emotional bandwidth may be shorter. We might be ignorant of our tone or response to others. (Remember how I was unkind about my friend's choice to diet?)

If this is your experience, have compassion for yourself. Your behavior while grieving is not a character flaw, but a symptom of grief.

What about Compassion for Others?

Many spiritual traditions describe developing compassion for others as a crucial element in the evolution of the person and the soul. But Witches, as a community, don't talk much about compassion, although it might serve us to do so. We spend a lot of time talking about blocking, shielding, setting boundaries, etc., all of which certainly have their place. Many of us are more adept at finding ways to separate ourselves from those who challenge us than exploring having compassion for these individuals. This may come from religious trauma, where some traditions may have encouraged us to unconditionally forgive abusers, which either left our own healing unaddressed or left us open to further harm. Because Witches are not always encouraged to forgive or have compassion for those who harm us, many rely on separation as a default response. Again, this certainly has its necessary place, particularly if we need to separate from abusive people or others with whom we simply can't get along. But a lack of compassion can also lead to cruelty, isolation, the destruction of Witchcraft communities, and a struggle to let go of past chapters and move on to new ones.

Compassion is not about excusing hurtful behavior from others or allowing our boundaries to be trampled on. Compassion can be many things, but it is most simply remembering that other people will make mistakes—not because they are bad people, but because they *are* people. Compassion reminds us not to take others' actions personally.

Still, having compassion for others while we are grieving may prove challenging. We are already emotionally exhausted. Trying to drum up compassion for others in these times can feel daunting. However, tapping a thread of compassion for others, even during our deepest grief, can make our own grief process gentler. Doing this, however, does not look like dismissing our feelings or allowing others to hurt us.

Not long after the miscarriage, I had a pregnant friend who took many opportunities to share the details of her pregnancy with me: her excitement, her plans, and more. I tried very hard to be kind about it. This was me showing compassion … right? I tried to recognize that the friend was excited and only wanted to draw me into her life and journey. I told myself that she probably felt she was giving me hope for my own situation by sharing the joy in hers. While I tried very hard to recognize her good intentions, every detail I heard reminded me of what I'd lost. Eventually, it became too much. I finally explained that while I was happy for her pregnancy, hearing so many details was quite painful for me and I needed a break from hearing about them. Apologetic and sympathetic, she promised that she understood and told me to take all the time that I needed.

The next day, however, I received an email invitation from her for her baby shower. I didn't know whether she'd chosen to invite me after our conversation, ignoring my feelings, or she wasn't mindful in double-checking her guest list before sending out the invite. I was devastated. Not only was I processing the reminder that I was not having a baby shower, I now felt unheard and misunderstood. When I told another friend how getting the invitation was even more hurtful given that I had just explained my situation to her, the other friend said, "She just wants you to feel included. She didn't mean to hurt you."

Of course, I *knew* that. I knew the pregnant friend meant well. But why was I, the grieving person, supposed to extend understanding to the well-intentioned but ultimately hurtful friend, as opposed to her needing to try to understand my situation? These well-intentioned people, the pregnant friend and the other friend trying to help me "see the other side," simply exacerbated my grief.

In addition to being expected to "get over it" and "move on," grieving people are also expected to graciously accept hurtful sentiments that others throw our way, particularly when they are well-intended. As grievers, we know that people are trying to help. We know they mean well. We know it's hard for them to see us hurting. We know. *We know. We KNOW.* But guess what? Others' feelings, misunderstandings, or mistakes in their approach to our grieving are not our problem to solve.

Another hard truth of grief is that the people who want most to help us are also the ones most likely to hurt us. People don't know what to say. They may spit out a hurtful trope à la "Everything happens for a reason." They may vanish. If they're a Witch, they may even tell us they've received a message from Spirit about our situation. They want to fill us with hope. Instead, they unintentionally salt our wounds.

In the first days after our loss, many texted asking if they could call. I would say yes, and we'd set a time. When that time would come around, however, I didn't always have the emotional bandwidth to pick up the phone. Seeing their name flash on the screen, however, was often all I needed. As it turned out, I didn't always need to talk. I simply needed to know that others were there.

But there were a few people in my life who literally vanished. These were people whom I'd had close to me in every big moment of my life, but when this devastating moment came around, they were not there. No calls, no cards, not even a text. When I would see them on Zoom calls or at social gatherings, they gave no indication that they were even aware of my loss, even though they knew it happened.

Does it matter that a few key people disappear from our lives when we need them, even as many others may step up? We may want to say no and talk ourselves into paying attention to the numbers of people who did come through, rather than the numbers who didn't. But relationships are not about numbers. A hundred cards from kind acquaintances do not fill the void of a life-long but absent friend.

Silences and disappearances can compound grief. If we've been in a strained place with a friend or relative and then experience a loss, we might think (or hope) that the loss will bring them back to us. But we may find that it doesn't. They may not come through. We may wonder if they care about us. We may feel resentful, thinking of times when we were there for them, perhaps feeling that our support was not reciprocated. Feeling ignored by those we love when we are grieving is a unique kind of hurt. The chances are good, though, that they are not ignoring us.

It's possible that something else is going on:

They don't know what to say: Many times, people vanish because they simply don't know what to say to us in our grief. Perhaps they are aware of the uncomfortable tropes and don't want to risk saying one accidentally. They may think it's better that they disappear than say the wrong thing.

They don't realize how important they are to you: This person may not realize their value to you and has no idea that their absence is painful.

They want to give you space: Many people want space while they are grieving, and some may believe that by disappearing from a grieving person's life, they are doing the right thing. This is a complicated concept. While many grieving people do need space, there are ways to show support without crowding them. (Sympathy cards were probably invented for this very reason!) At worst, leaning into "giving them space" is an easy out. It's less effort for the person who disappears and makes them appear supportive.

At the same time, it may be that people who vanish during tough times truly believe this is the best thing they can offer you. Maybe they personally like being alone while they grieve. Maybe they don't trust themselves to show up in a way that's helpful for you. Maybe they simply don't know what to do. They vanish because they don't believe their presence can help you. It may not be true, but they may not know that.

They're waiting for you to come to them: When I mentioned to one of the absent friends that it was hard to not hear from them in those early days, they said they were waiting for me to come to them. They had worried that by reaching out to me, they would remind me of the loss and upset me if I was having a good day. It didn't occur to them that there was no way to remind me of the loss, as it wasn't something I could forget, and that there are no good days to ruin in the aftermath of a severe loss.

The "waiting for you to come to me" is another complicated sentiment, as again, it puts work on the grieving person. But sometimes, our loved ones truly are waiting for a sign from us. While it's not our job to give them a sign, their absence isn't necessarily a sign that they don't care.

Chances are, you already knew all of this and don't need a reminder: Grieving people aren't dense to the root of the foibles of fumbling loved ones. We know they mean well. We know they're trying. We know that many are expecting us to educate them on how to best support us. But when certain people vanish, it may call us to reconsider our relationships with them.

Perhaps you are someone who wants lots of space and don't mind the absence. Or, you may be someone who craves company while you are grieving, and the absence of loved ones is particularly painful. Many people want something in between. The process of grief churns and changes, and what we need one day will be radically different from what we need on the next. We may not want to talk every day. We may not want to see people a lot. But many of us like to know that people are there when we're ready for their company. Some people won't be. And others may encourage us to give them a pass. "They just don't know what to do …" is what you're likely to hear, and yes, it may be true. But it doesn't stop the sting.

Compassion is not about giving people "a pass." Compassion is about giving ourselves better space to heal.

Grief naturally makes us more compassionate. We find ourselves more understanding of the pain of others. We may find ourselves defending those whose pain is dismissed by others. Part of this growth of compassion after a loss occurs when others unintentionally walk on our feelings as we grieve. Being open and sensitive in our time of grief, we recognize that the people who love us are honestly trying to help, but the injuries of the well-intentioned persons remain.

Compassion Does Not Have to Look Like This

- Smiling, nodding, and ignoring unhelpful comments such as "They're in a better place," "The universe has a plan," or "They wouldn't want you to be sad."

- Making space for and giving information to "tragedy voyeurs," such as the classmate from high school you haven't spoken to in years who suddenly appears in your DMs asking for all the details about the flood that washed away your home and town. "So...how deep was the mud? How long did you wait on your roof?" They may promise they're being supportive, while it's obvious that they're getting a thrill from your story, and may be garnering attention by relaying it to others. These tragedy voyeurs may lap up every gory detail of your tragic loss...but they'll be the last ones to help you rebuild.
- Accepting energy, messages, or other "spiritual" gifts from people to "help" you when you don't want them.
- Attending social gatherings out of obligation when you're not ready because you don't want to hurt the feelings of the nice person who invited you.
- Listening to or comforting the person making your loss about them: "You don't know how hard your breakup was for me...I loved you two so much as a couple..."
- Pretending everything is fine when the close friend who vanished after your loss comes back into your life pretending your loss never happened.

Many of us are conditioned to stay quiet when our feelings are hurt. We're encouraged to be polite, to avoid conflict, and (again) to see where the other person is coming from. Many of us may mistake this as being compassionate when it's more about making others comfortable at the cost of our own comfort.

Calling out hurtful behavior and potentially making the situation uncomfortable is itself an act of compassion. If the person spouting a hurtful trope truly wanted to be helpful, wouldn't they want to know that there is a better way for them to be helpful?

Compassion for Others May Look Like This

- Saying, "I know you mean well, but hearing that 'They're in a better place' [or fill in the blank with whatever they said] is very hurtful."
- Being mindful of who you share information with, such as ignoring "tragedy voyeurs" and therefore not feeding their problematic behavior, or even responding with, "Thank you for your concern; I'm not in a good place to share this information." Also, it's okay to block these people for a time … or forever!
- Responding with, "Thank you for inviting me, but I need more time before I start being social again. I'll let you know when I'm ready to be on future invite lists."
- Saying to the person who is upset about your loss, "I hear that you're struggling with this, but I'm not in a place to help you. You'll probably get better support from a different friend or even a mental health professional."
- "I recognize that you didn't mean to hurt me, but it was very hard not hearing from you for so long."

These could be described as setting healthy boundaries, and yes, that's true. However, setting boundaries is its own act of compassion—for both the other party and ourselves.

At the same time, you may not have the immediate energy to educate people on how to care for you in your grief. Remember, grief uses an extreme amount of energy. Even if our loss isn't on our mind's forefront, it is draining. After having a heart-to-heart with my pregnant friend but still receiving a baby shower invitation, I didn't have the energy to explain to her why I didn't want to go … or why her choice to invite me (although surely well-meaning) was painful. Instead, I chose to take compassionate space from this friend. I did not attend the baby shower, and when she came to me for advice on another matter a month later, I told her gently that I was struggling and was not the right person for her to consult. I assured her I cared for her, but for the health of myself and our friendship, I needed time. She kindly accepted my request, and we remain friends to this day.

There is compassion in the choice to take space from the people who drain us while we are grieving. We could lash out at them. We could write them off as terrible, insensitive people. Or we can make the compassionate choice to recognize that while they may mean well, they are not the people we need around us now. Taking distance from relationships you'd like to preserve is itself a great act of compassion and a wonderful gift you are giving yourself and the people in your life—whether they know it or not!

Now, this is not a perfect model. It doesn't fit every situation. A sad truth about grief is that it can bring out others' cruelty too. There are people who will laugh at the pain of others. They deliberately, or even publicly, minimize it. Within our own Witchcraft communities, I've seen people post on social media that a certain grieving person "deserved" the sorrow they're experiencing. As angry as I've been with others—and even with as many people I am at odds with in this world—I cannot imagine publicly ridiculing, shaming, or applauding someone's grief. No matter how much I might dislike the person, I can and do recognize when they are grieving and offer them the compassion and respect they deserve.

Still, there are those who will use the opportunity to hurt a grieving person. If this happens to you, you may have a better time finding compassion for them down the road. You may view their cruel behavior as the result of their own trauma, a gross lack of understanding, or otherwise. Grief can, and does, trigger the grief of others. Sometimes grieving people can be the unkindest to other grievers. You may know and understand all of this. But you do not *need* to be the "bigger person" in these situations. If someone is cruel to you in the wake of your grief, you have a right to be angry, scared, sad, or otherwise. While I do not think the drop-block-shield tactic should be the default response to every conflict, there are times when it is warranted. You have the right to block or cut someone off if their behavior is unduly unkind. For your own energy's sake, do not get into a fight with them about why you deserve your grief. (Chances are that a fight is exactly what they want from you.) Remove yourself from their vicinity if you are able. Call in support from those who you know will be there for you.

Grieving around other humans is a constant game of choice: the choice of whether to share our journey, and the choice of who we share it with, all while opening ourselves up to unintended hurts from those who don't know how to treat us while we grieve. We will find ourselves choosing which relationships to maintain, which to take a break from, and sometimes, which ones we'll have to discontinue. Not all relationships will survive grief, and they don't have to. The choice of which relationships to maintain and which to let go is entirely yours, but remember to have compassion for yourself as you make these choices. You are not mean or petty if you need to change the landscape of your relationships in the wake of your loss.

Resentment Does Not Protect You

Resentment is the nasty sidekick of grief. It shows up uninvited and whispers into our ears that not only are we the only ones feeling the grief, the whole world is happy and we're not. In fact, the world is being happy *at* us. It's happy-ing on purpose, solely to make us feel worse.

At least, that's how things may feel.

Grief can make us take things personally, including and especially things that don't have anything to do with us. Shortly after our loss, a different pregnant friend of mine posted on Twitter: "Be nice to women who are nine months pregnant. They are in AGONY!"

I was furious. How dare she complain about being nine months pregnant? Didn't she know how many people would love to be in her situation? Even though she had no idea I'd recently lost my own pregnancy, I was personally offended that she would complain in a format where I would see it. "Perhaps you're not in as much agony as someone who just lost their baby—" I started to respond before deleting it.

Was it wrong for my friend to share her story? Of course not. Was her pain real? Absolutely. Had she posted it to hurt me? Also no. Grief, and its buddy Resentment, like to tell us that other people are happy, and because of that, we are sad. Grief wants us to believe that there are a finite number of blessings in the world, that we were given loss because someone else was given joy. We start to blame other people, even unconsciously, for being happy while we are grieving, as though they are responsible.

It. Is. Not. True.

Even amid our grief, my husband and I have had happy times. We took trips. We loved our dog and our cats. We have the coolest house. We're not without our challenges, but we're dorky and funny and genuinely enjoy each other's company. Sometimes, I post on social media about something fun we've done together or something hilarious my husband said. Is this specifically to hurt people who are lonely, going through a divorce, or unhappy in their relationships? Of course not. You may even be reading this and not feel great about it, but I didn't write any of this with the intention of causing you hurt. Witchcraft reminds us that while we may all be connected, multiple realities can exist. My friend can be happy about having a child and unhappy about being nine-months pregnant. At the same time, I can be sad about my own situation and not especially sympathetic to her plight, while also recognizing that her sharing her story was not a deliberate affront to me. What I consciously tried to remember is that my baby did not die because her baby lived. The universe is not doling out a limited number of blessings. We do not suffer because someone else is thriving, just as we do not thrive because someone else suffers.

At the same time, you do not have to force yourself to be happy for others who are experiencing joy when you are experiencing loss. If you are going through a painful breakup, you don't have to attend the friend's wedding or anniversary party. If you are struggling with the loss of a parent, maybe you're not up for hearing about Mother's or Father's Day plans, or even more so, you're not up for hearing someone complain about an argument they're having with their living parent. But for our own healing purposes, we must remember that people are not experiencing joy in these spaces *because* we are experiencing grief in them. They are not having their celebrations *at* us.

Grief wants us to believe that others are experiencing joy in front of us on purpose. While it would be great if good things could only happen to others when we're feeling better in our grief process, it's impossible. The world will continue, and things will happen to other people, both good and bad. Taking others' joys as a personal affront further complicates grief and causes more pain. It's an insult to the self, added to an already painful injury.

Remembering that other lives and joys exist amid our grief is itself a great act of compassion. It's not about being a nice person at the cost of our own feelings. We don't have to take part in the celebrations of others' joy if we're not ready, but we can consciously avoid resenting others' joy. Compassion removes those pieces of pain that make our grief process more cumbersome. Not everyone knows what we are going through. They are not trying to harm us by living their lives. In truth, there may be more grief in their lives than we know.

When I stopped being angry at the gods long enough to stand at their altar, my morning devotion was simply, "Help me today to be kind to others. Also, help me today to be kind to myself."

Being unkind to myself has looked like me blaming myself for the losses I've experienced, replaying the scariest parts of these losses in my mind, and having arguments with myself from the past. It has also meant rehashing the hurtful, even if well-meaning, comments of others and having hypothetical arguments with people who I assumed might say trite, hurtful tropes … someday. I reminded myself that others are human, as am I. When it was hard to ask the gods for much of anything, I found that I could still ask the gods for compassion for others, as well as myself.

Grief is hard. We deserve to be treated gently—by others, as well as ourselves. Resentment is an easy emotional space to slip into, but it ultimately hurts us even more. Compassion can help us acknowledge and dismantle resentment when it appears, leaving us more space to focus on processing our grief.

Rituals of Compassion: Air and Fire

Depending on what your needs are, this series of rituals may help you address different areas of your life with different needs.

A Ritual to Communicate Needs Using the Power of Air

Consider doing a smoke cleansing using rosemary, lavender, or another accessible herb that you find cleansing and healing. Use the smoke to cleanse your home of misconceptions and unwanted words. If you're not sure what your needs are, use the smoke to help clarify what your needs might be. A suggested incantation for this is below:

> *Winds of healing, I welcome thee.*
> *Air of clearing, I embrace thee.*
> *Wisps and whispers, I fear you not.*
> *Words of comfort and home, change is brought.*

When the smoke has gone out, consider snipping a few pieces from the herbs you used to smoke cleanse and carry them in a sachet with you when out and about.

If you live in a place where you cannot use smoke, you have an allergy, or you simply don't want smoke in your house, soak a few plants commonly used in smoke clearings (such as lavender, rosemary, or cedar) in a bowl of water and sprinkle it around your home or space to create the same desired effect.

A Ritual to Align Fury Using the Power of Fire

When you are feeling such rage that you are unable to focus on other things, it may be time to allocate that rage to something else. It's often said that anger is a screen over injury, and anger is a natural byproduct of loss and grief. The challenge is not to automatically extinguish it, but to sit with the anger and look deeply at it, understanding its source and its many parts.

Like fire, anger is best used when directed at a purpose. When left unchecked, like fire, it can consume us and those around us. When we better understand what fuels our anger, we can navigate it for our best use instead of letting it consume us.

When you are ready to sit with your anger, take a candle (flame or battery-operated) and bring it to your magick space or a private space. Light (or turn on) the flame.

Speak to the flame. List the things that anger you now, whether related to your loss or not. Don't try to justify or explain your anger. This is not the time to include, "I shouldn't be angry … but …" Just as there are no rules about what "should" and "shouldn't" burn, on the grief journey there are no rules about what "should" or "shouldn't" anger you.

After you have sat with the flame for a while, imagine pinning the things that anger you to the flame. What does the anger look like when it's outside of you? Now that you've seen it, what do you want to do with it? What actions do you want to take? Are there measures of comforting yourself you'd like to embrace? Again, this is not necessarily about pushing to rid yourself of anger. The anger will leave you when it's ready. Ultimately, the goal is to simply look at the anger from another perspective.

Let the flame burn while you are with it. Do not leave the flame unattended. When the flame has burned itself out, thank its remnants for their support of your work. If you are a journal-keeper, this is a great time to write down your reflections and observations about your anger.

Blame and Shame

Blame grows in the loss, like weeds in the broken bricks or pavement. When we run out of people to blame, we blame ourselves. When we've run out of things to blame on ourselves, we blame the gods. Order of events may vary.

A couple of months after we lost our baby, I was finally in a place in my grieving journey where I felt comfortable discussing next steps: how my husband and I might build our family, as well as closing some avenues we had decided not to explore. I shared my thoughts with a friend, but they misunderstood what I was trying to say. They offered a long, well-meaning, but unintentionally insensitive slab of advice ... but one that felt like a hug across a surgical wound. I ended our call shaking and ran to the kitchen, in too many tears to speak. My husband was washing dishes and tried to piece together what had just happened, but I was too upset to explain. A nurse in his professional life, he stared with the measured, observant eye of a medical person, but I didn't want to be observed. I didn't have a name for what I needed. Before the loss, I might have found comfort at one of the many altars in our house, but not then. The gods and ancestors still felt far and empty. The walls were closing in again, and I felt so much rage that I feared I might smash things in our beloved home.

I went out into the damp night and sat on the wet grass.

Before our loss, I gave morning offerings to the land spirits in the form of water, rice, seeds, removal of invasive weeds, replanting native plants, or simply being present and marveling at the beauty of a young day. After the loss, this was the one ritual I had not cast aside. In these rituals, I don't ask the land spirits for anything, and that night was no different. I didn't ask for peace or healing. I didn't try to banish my anger or try to formulate words to better articulate it. I simply sat in that natural space. And breathed.

If grief were a clean and linear process, I might label that night as when I came back to Witchcraft, but that wouldn't be accurate. On that cold, angry night, I still wasn't sure about the presence of gods, the efficacy of magick, or the point of ancestor worship. But I found a moment of comfort in the natural world. I slipped out of a head packed with jagged thoughts and eased into the rhythm of the planet. If there is anything to being a Witch, maybe that's it.

I didn't return to practicing Witchcraft that night. But for the first time since our loss, I thought I might still be a Witch.

"When the Hard Space Remains"

I see you fighting. I see you trying.
I feel you keeping the work quiet, to keep the burden off
    others
To give yourself a break from feeling
I hear you trying to laugh, when you don't remember how
I see you smiling at a misspent well wish
I see you praying to sleep through the night and failing,
    again.
I see you waiting through the thin hours of the night,
maybe pacing the house,
maybe twisting in bed.
I see you trying to walk through life again,
and limping home when it's too hard.
I see you.

—**Courtney Weber**

6

Grieving Without Closure

Closure.

Ugh.

The desire for closure is the reason most of my tarot clients book readings. "Why did they leave?" "Why did they die?" "Will I ever get answers?" are common questions. Some are more direct: "Will I ever get closure?" The question makes me cringe, but I also deeply empathize. I've asked that same question many times myself—of other readers and of my own tired tarot deck. My own need for closure has kept me up many, many nights. Wanting closure is yet one more thing that makes us human.

Human beings crave answers. We've created whole religions and ideologies around finding answers to such nebulous questions. Some might even argue that we have invented whole pantheons simply to answer the wrenching question: "Why did it happen?"

When we lose, we want it to mean something. The pain needs to be worth it. It's too great to *not* have a story attached. Many religions lean into "It was God's plan," or in Witchcraft communities, many are quick to say something like, "It was destiny." Our losses can be easier to accept if there is a purpose attached: "They went to a better place," "The spouse left because we are meant for something better," or my least favorite, "The gods willed it." These quips and platitudes can be infuriating to hear, but believing there is a greater purpose attached to the loss is easier to accept than the possibility that there was no purpose at all. It's harder to accept that the partner simply didn't love us enough to stay, that the death was random, or our place of employment simply didn't value us when they let us go. There *must* be a purpose, right? We often believe that finding that purpose will enable us to have closure, and that closure is the one key to healing.

There is nothing inherently wrong with wanting closure. But one of the painful things about closure is that it rarely appears in a neat, acceptable package, if it even appears at all. When my last relationship ended, I had a recurring dream of a phone call to my former lover, calling from a corded landline such as the one in my childhood home. In the dream, I screamed, "Why? Why? Why?" He would respond, but the line was too crackled for me to understand him. The call always dropped at the end of the dream, without me getting an answer.

"My goodness," my therapist said when I told her about the dream as she tried to conceal a chuckle. "That dream really explains itself."

The dream was telling me a hard truth: I would never get an answer as to why the relationship ended. When we broke up, he offered a list of the usual relationship-ending suspects: Wanting something else, needing to focus on himself, realizing there were things in his past he needed to face, etc., etc. At the time, I believed none of them. I wanted there to be some grander reason for why he ended the relationship. I spun and clung to stories about him wanting to be with me but being scared. I armchair diagnosed him with a slew of mental illnesses and believed that if he got treatment for them, he would see clearly that being with me was best. I sought countless tarot readings to find out if our love had been cursed by a jealous third party. I needed not just a reason to explain why the relationship failed, but a reason I could accept. I told myself it was me wanting closure. Ultimately, I wanted the closure to come from him, by him telling me why he'd left … and that answer would be one I felt comfortable accepting.

Eventually, when the grief spiral had done its work and I could see the loss with objectivity, I accepted the truth: he simply didn't want to be with me. The truth was there all along, and when I was finally ready to accept it, the acceptance was its own closure. It didn't come from him. It came from me.

A few years later, while I was reading tarot at an event in New York City, I fielded the same plethora of questions I typically got at such events: "When will I meet someone?" "Should I change jobs?" "Are they 'the one'?" But toward the end of the night, a young woman with a kind smile came to my table. We were surely of a similar age, but her eyes were tired, as though she'd seen much more in her years than I had. She asked, "Why were my parents murdered?"

For years, I derided myself over the answer I gave her. Horrified by her situation and terrified to tell her something that would make her more upset, I declined to answer her question. I explained that my cards were not equipped to see a "why" for something like that. Instead, I suggested she ask the cards for help navigating her healing after such a devastating loss. She politely agreed, but inside, I felt sick. Had I made her grief worse by not answering her question? Did she feel abandoned? Was I the worst tarot reader of all time? After reading for her, I folded up my table-cloth for the night even though I was still scheduled for another hour. I couldn't take another question that night. (An artist at the event, who overheard the question and my response, asked for the cloth as he wanted to use it in an installation on grief that he was creating. I agreed and gave it to him. To this day, I hope this artist will find me and show me what he did with the cloth.)

I left that night ashamed of veering away from that question, thinking that I could have helped this grieving woman more if I had at least tried to look at the "whys." But now, I feel better about the decision. It was not my place to tell this woman why this hor-rific thing happened. It wasn't anyone's place. The horrible, hard truth is that there was likely no reason. Most of all, the journey to closure was one she could only take alone.

Closure Is a Myth

Something being a myth does not mean that it's false. On the Witchcraft path, many of us look to the myths of gods, plants, landscapes, or otherwise not as scientific truths but as stories that can help us better understand their nature. A myth is a beautiful thing. The power of story is one of the things that makes human beings wonderful. There is not a corner of the world where stories and myths do not help us understand existence. Myths are gauzy and malleable, and some contain pieces of facts, but which of the myths' pieces are factual is often shrouded in mystery. Myths only become problematic when they are treated like irrefutable truths, such as when some Christian sects in the United States cling to the Bible's creation story as factual while disregarding the science of the origins of the world, using these beliefs to influence public education. Without allowing myth its inspirational nature and attempting to shape it into concrete fact, myths become oppressive and dangerous.

Still, the creation of myth is as natural to human experience as craving closure. We want to understand outcomes. While many of us rail against spoilers in movies and books, we can't stand it if we haven't seen the end ourselves. I readily admit that I started reading tarot to find out how certain situations would end, particularly if I was anxious about them. When loss happens, we desperately crave answers as to why. When we cannot get answers from others, we create them through stories.

Stories help us make sense of terrible or confusing things. Naturally, we also want stories for our loss. We may develop a grand myth about our loss so that it will mean something, but we also want it to be one hundred percent true. But just as it's harmful for a religion to change school curriculum to support a myth they wish to make factual, we harm ourselves when we attempt to prove our loss's story as factual. This proof may seem to provide the closure we crave, and through this closure, we may think we will find peace. But doing this is akin to keeping ourselves locked in a cage and waiting for someone to unlock the door … when all the while the key was in our hand.

Not all myths contain fact, and not all losses will have an explanation. The greatest but hardest truth about closure is that it will never come from outside of ourselves. No one can create closure but us.

An Exercise for Revering Loss Without Closure

Write the story of your loss in a manner as matter of fact as possible, using as few opinions or descriptors as you can. Imagine a computer were describing the events, e.g., "Person described as 'partner' sleeps and brushes teeth in a different house" or "Woman aged ninety-five stopped breathing and heart discontinued beating and all signs of described biological life ceased."

Now, write about your loss as though it were a myth. Make it as fantastical as you want. For example, "Gallant prince rode off with the snow queen and now lives in a palace of ice" or "Door to alternate dimension opened in hospital room. Mimaw got off the bed, fixed her hair, and walked through it."

Don't create an ending for this story. Experience it without an ending. See its beauty without a "why" attached.

Try reading both versions aloud to yourself or a trusted person in a sacred space. Allow yourself to feel whatever comes up, or doesn't. Again, this is not the time to judge or analyze the situation or how you are responding to it, if you are responding at all. Simply observe where you are right now in this process.

Afterward, create space for yourself to let the feelings flow. Examples might be listening to a beloved playlist while you cry, taking a walk while you rage, cooking something delicious, or cleaning a part of your home if you feel restless.

Try this exercise several times, writing the story in different ways, but don't include a "why." Just experience the story without it. The story will still be powerful without the "why" attached.

Even after reaching a place of acceptance, a myth will have a mystery. The truth of my breakup story was that he didn't want to be with me. The mystery is that I don't know why. But I don't need or want to know. I have closure, not because my story was verified by my former love, but because I created and accepted the closure on my own.

Ambiguous Loss: A Mean Kind of Loss

Perhaps more than any loss, ambiguous loss craves closure. Ambiguous loss, or loss that isn't defined, is an uncomfortable and yet terribly common experience that perhaps doesn't get enough attention. An example of this is when someone "ghosts": that is, a friend or romantic person suddenly removes themselves from your life. They don't return your texts, they're cordial but distant in public spaces, or maybe they won't even speak to you, and you don't know why. The person is still alive, but they're no longer part of your life.

Other ambiguous losses include fertility treatments that didn't work. While there is no official loss to mourn, the loss of potential is its own grief journey. Another example is someone who is physically alive but through diseases like dementia or Alzheimer's, or through extreme substance use, the person they once were isn't there anymore.

One of the most heartbreaking ambiguous losses is when a loved one goes missing and is presumed deceased. As I write this, it has been eleven months since an old friend of mine was last seen. She is presumed to be deceased, but there is no way to verify that, and therefore, mourning is tough. Do we hold a memorial service for her, even though there is no body? Does that sunset all hope in the very slim possibility that she might reappear again? At what point do I, as a Witch, add her to the altar of my beloved dead?

In these cases and others, grief can be stuck like a rollercoaster paused before the first big hill. We're scared, but we're stuck. We know the real pain is coming when the loss is finally verified, but what do we do with the wrenching anticipation? Can we mourn if we can't point to the loss? How do we move forward when the last chapter isn't officially over? It's in moments like these we desperately crave closure, and it seems far away.

Many Witches believe in something called the astral plane. The definition of the astral plane varies among different traditions and philosophies, but a very basic definition might be that it's a spiritual meeting place, composed of the spirits of people, animals, and even plants and interdimensional beings. Some of these souls are of deceased beings, some are on their way to being born or reincarnated, and some are living beings who wind up on the astral plane during meditation or even dreams. Among many things, the astral plane is also a place where we can connect with living people we may not be able to speak with in waking life. The astral plane appears differently for each person. For me, it can appear in the form of an amusement park sitting by a body of water. I've run into many friends there in dreams who have later confirmed that they had similar dreams around the same time. Sometimes, I've seen it as a wide meadow. Other times, a dark forest. A few times, it's a simple white room with no furniture, sound, or otherwise. On the astral, I've had hard conversations with people that I couldn't have had in waking life, either because of logistics or distance, or because things were too fraught between us to have a productive discussion.

Connecting with people on the astral plane can be extremely healing during ambiguous loss. This is a deeper, more spiritual version of the "write them a letter and never send it," which also has its merits, but for many people is not as satisfying. We want the experience of saying what's on our mind and heart in the presence of the person whom we want to hear it. If we can't do that in person, we can do it with our spirits.

An Exercise for Exploring the Astral Plane

If you are someone who remembers your dreams, take note of recurring locations in them. Some common astral dream visit locations include airports, highways, subway tunnels, or even shopping malls. Other versions include childhood homes, meadows, palaces, or fantastical sites. Some people dream of going to a library or to outer space. If you have recurring dreams in a specific place, this may be the setting of your access point to the astral plane.

If you are not someone who remembers your dreams, create some time to meditate on or imagine what a spiritual meeting space might look like for you. Maybe you love forests, and so imagining yourself in a sunlit or snowy forest might do the trick. If you're a lover of libraries, imagine one that sings to your book-loving soul. It can be big and grand or tiny and cozy, like a small living room with a roaring fireplace. There are no wrong answers.

Whether you're recalling this image from a dream or from your imagination, find a quiet space and time to envision this place. Many people like to do this in a sacred space, such as next to their altars. I have also found success doing this while in bed, on a plane, or riding in a car. (Not while driving, of course!) Once you are there, call forth the person or persons you want to speak to. Once you see them in your mind (or imagine the feeling of their physical presence if you struggle with visualization), open your heart. Let everything pour out.

Whether these are words of kindness or cruelty, heartbreak or rage, or simply exhaustion, describe your feelings, confusion, or otherwise. If this is a deceased person you did not get a chance to say goodbye to, you can tell them everything you loved about them and how much you miss them, or even address some unfinished, uncomfortable business. This latter part is a good exercise for people who are still living but with whom you may not be able to speak.

Whatever you choose to say, wherever you choose to say it, be as open and honest as possible. You do not need to edit or be polite. Say what needs to be said. Ask the questions you need to ask. Take time and listen, but don't force the vision of the other person to respond. Simply be open to what they say in return, which may surprise you. They may not say anything now, but you may dream of their response at another time or even receive it in another way, such as in a reading or through synchronicity.

This exercise bears repeating a few times. Particularly if the heartbreak was deep or the relationship was long, there may be many things you'll want to discuss with the other person. You can bring them the same questions and feelings numerous times. This is your process. Do the work as many times as you feel it is appropriate.

Don't use this time to wish the other person pain and suffering, even if that's what they caused you. Cursing absolutely has its place, but this particular work is about your healing, not them getting what they may rightfully deserve. Even if the curse is warranted, cursing another person before doing at least some healing work on yourself can create a spiritual mess. One, you may be so exhausted from your grief that your curse is ineffective. Two, cursing can also keep you connected to the curse's target when what might be best for you is to separate energetically. Three, your feelings (although valid!) might prompt you to do an overly intense curse that might cause some steep imbalances in your own life, ones which might require additional magickal or personal work to correct. A good guideline for this work: Heal first. If the need still exists, curse later.

Through this work, simply relaying your feelings and asking questions can go a long way to your own process of healing and creating closure after ambiguous loss. However, if you prefer to speak in person and can do so, go for it! But this practice is good when the person is no longer accessible to you or if things are so fraught that a conversation can't be had.

Loss on Our Terms Is Still Loss

When I broke up with my first serious boyfriend, I was surprised by how upset *I* was, even though I was the one who ended it. Although I knew I would eventually be happier without him, I had complicated feelings: missing the familiarity of our relationship, guilt at the pain my leaving had caused him, even some impending jealousy knowing that he would eventually meet someone else. I thought that perhaps I shouldn't mourn because I was the one who caused the loss. But my own grief was real and valid. Loss on our terms is still loss. Maybe we move for our dream job, but we struggle with leaving our former home. Maybe we chose to end the relationship, but we will still mourn what we no longer have with them. The loss may be on our terms, but it is still loss. Grief will still follow.

We can't circumvent suffering, even when we choose to lose. We may fear the grief of the loss before it happens more than we experience it when the loss happens.

A Water Ritual in Preparation
to Lose Something by Choice

Bath rituals are incredibly powerful and healing, and they needn't be complicated either. A few particularly helpful ingredients for this specific work may already be in your kitchen cabinet. If not, they are easily found at a grocery store:

- Apple cider vinegar
- Salt (sea salt, kosher salt, or table salt)
- Lavender (a bag of lavender tea is fine)
- Lemon juice or lemon slices
- Bay leaf (The bay leaf can either be added to the bath or burned prior to stepping into the bath and the smoke used for a smoke cleansing.)

Once you've added these ingredients to your bath, settle in and focus on what you are choosing to lose. If you don't have a bathtub, place these ingredients in a pot of water. Boil for a few minutes, strain out the herbs, and let the water cool until it is warm or even tepid. Bring the warm or tepid (not boiling) water into the shower and use it to bathe yourself.

You may want to consider lighting a candle. I like to turn out all the lights in my bathroom and sit with only the light of a burning candle. No matter how you get comfortable, take the time to acknowledge what you're about to lose. If it's a relationship, consider speaking to the person in your mind or on the astral plane and explaining what you are about to do and why. If it's leaving a place, a community, or something else altogether, imagine a single figure (a person, animal, or entity) that represents it. Don't limit your feelings or criticize yourself for feeling them. This is your place to mourn.

When you have said all that you need to say, release the water down the drain, allowing yourself to envision the person or entity moving away from you, in peace, with the water.

Not only will this ritual help you with separating from the person or the situation, it will also potentially help the other party, on a spiritual level, prepare for your departure, even if they don't know it's coming.

Closure after the Loss of a Relationship

In some ways, the death of a loved one is a clean kind of loss. We have a specific focus point for our grief: the person who is no longer alive. Moreover, we are likely to find more support from such a loss. Others are likely to understand the grief we experience after a grandparent dies, but how many will understand the complicated grief we feel if they are technically still alive but age or illness has changed their personality into one we don't recognize? Many Witches leave their families of origin after abuse or trauma. These people may still be alive, and while it may technically be better to be distant from them, there can be grief in losing those people. In many cases, there is grief in losing a family one never had.

In many ways, ambiguous loss is a more complicated grieving process. When we lose someone we love but that person is still living, we're likely to process anger, maybe even jealousy. We may still share friends or even relatives with the living person we lost, and we may wish others could better understand our perspective or take our side. We may question our decisions, particularly if we are pressured by others to make amends that we do not want to make. If they are the one who left us, we may crave an answer as to why. These nagging questions and feelings can make this kind of ambiguous grief even more difficult.

What Does Closure Mean to You?

When my tarot clients ask if they'll ever get closure with an ex or a former friend, or a reason as to why something happened, I hand them a question of my own: "What does closure mean to you?"

Closure is an infuriatingly subjective term. It means something different to each of us. For some, closure may be a heartfelt apology from the person who harmed us, but will we ever get it? And if we get the apology, will it be genuine? What if that apology takes twenty years to come to us? Are we going to keep our own healing on pause for a lifetime? And if it does come and it is heartfelt, will it undo the pain we already endured?

Others may crave an honest explanation. In *Kill Bill: Vol. 2*, one of my favorite movies, Bill finds his closure by inventing a "truth serum": a concoction he shoots into his former lover's knee, which forces her to truthfully explain why she left him. When I first saw the film, I was fresh off my breakup and wild with jealousy over Bill's ability to get such an answer from his former lover. In time, I realized that the movie took such a fantastical approach to getting the truth because in real life, we are rarely going to get the answers we seek, even if we ask for them directly. Maybe the other person doesn't want to answer. Maybe they fear hurting us further. Maybe they don't want to look like the villain. Maybe they themselves don't even know. Maybe they will tell us the truth, but it's not what we want to hear.

Perhaps most painful are the times when there is no one to answer the questions. Why did the forest fire devour *my* town? Why did the cancer pick *my* parent? Why did the pandemic choose *my* lifetime? It's those nebulous answers, or the lack of answers, that can make us rage with the craving for closure.

Closure is something we create for ourselves. When we place our closure in the hands of others, real or imagined, it won't come. And we will suffer.

Nowhere is this perhaps truer than in the loss of a friend. Friendships can and often do carry more emotional weight and intimacy than most romantic relationships, but their endings can be frayed and tangled. It's rare to have a friendship breakup moment in the way that we might with a romantic partner. More often, friendships fade and change. One day we may simply realize the friend isn't there anymore, even without someone saying, "It's over." In these days of social media, deleting someone or being deleted from someone's friend or follower list is the closest thing to a breakup conversation that most of us will have with a friend. But still, questions are likely to remain after the ending of a friendship. The loss of a friend is something deeply underestimated and under-recognized. More so than even the dissolution of the romantic relationship, the conclusion of a friendship (whether you initiated that conclusion or not) requires the self-directed act of closure.

If this is your experience, consider doing the water ritual mentioned above, even if this happens after the friendship has ended. Or have a conversation with them on the astral plane. But before doing any rituals for closure, ask yourself what kind of closure you seek. Is this a friendship you never wish to revisit? Is it the kind of friendship you would welcome at another time? If they ended it, let them know if they are welcome to return. If you do not wish to ever revisit the friendship, let them know that. This can be especially important if you are not on speaking terms with this person.

Keep in mind that rarely does closure come in one conversation, one ritual, one moment. Even if each of us were lucky enough to get an honest, true answer as to "why did it happen?", we won't get closure until we decide for ourselves that the closure has taken place. Closure doesn't mean we forget what we suffered. Closure can mean that we accept what happened, and that we are unlikely to get all the answers we seek, and that some answers may not exist. Remember, just as there is mystery in myth, there will be mystery in your story too. The mystery is part of what makes your story beautiful and sacred. Honoring that mystery may be the first step to closure, and your own closure can be a first step to peace.

(Content warning: This next section includes a reference to a suicide. To skip past this section, please turn to page 123.)

Witchcraft and Surrender

Here's the thing…when you're dealing with something like grief and trauma, I'm not sure Witchcraft is the right technology to lean into. Witchcraft is more about controlling your destiny, but there are many times in life when you have to surrender. Sometimes I feel as though Witchcraft is better as a preventative, perhaps a way to bolster yourself so that when those inevitable times come, you're better able to withstand them. But when you're actually going through grief, I'm not sure Witchcraft is the best thing. As an atheist Witch, I turn to intense psychotherapy, bodywork, things like that. When it comes to deep, heavy trauma, sometimes surrender is what you have to do, and Witchcraft is not big on surrender! While it really depends on the Witch, I do think there needs to be something beyond ritual. Ritual work is saying, "I cannot surrender to this. That's why I'm going to do ritual." For me, the surrender is having a good therapist. But for some people, surrender could be getting on your knees and praying.

More than ten years ago, I lost the person that I was in a romantic relationship with, who perhaps I was going to marry. I lost him to suicide. It was very sudden and violent. Violent death is different because there's no time for goodbyes. Witches can sometimes be disgustingly "Get over it" or "Positivity only," but Witches are supposed to be in touch with the unseen realms. Traditionally, Witches were known to be necromancers. They were the ones believed to get in touch with the spirits of the dead, and yet, so many modern Witches don't honor that tradition. They don't honor this entire, invisible, dead world, which is unfortunate. I believe a Witch is a liminal creature who straddles life and death, dreams and awake times. That's the entire point of magick—to be in the in-between spaces.

When tragedy hits, no ritual will create a shortcut through your grief. There is no tea ceremony to hack your way through it. There is no guru who can take on the pain of walking through that fire. And at that point, the Witch, the atheists, the Christians, we're the same. We're one hundred percent the same as our ancestors a hundred thousand years ago on the savanna in Africa, facing down a lion who's about to eat them. It's easy to be a Witch when you're surrounded by air conditioning and fluffy pillows. But can you still be a Witch when you're faced with this man-eating lion, figurative or literal? To be honest, that's when you become a real Witch. A lot of grieving people think they've lost their faith (in the wake of grief). But they come back to it, and when they do, it's deep. It's unshakable.

~**Chaweon Koo**

7

The Gifts of Grief

"Every cloud has a silver lining" is yet another platitude that is not particularly helpful to many grieving people. It generally means, "For every crappy thing that happens, there is a bright side!" So … there's something good about the heartbreaking thing that we lost? To many grieving folks, that is highly doubtful.

What is good about the silver linings of clouds anyway? Does it mean the rain is going to stop? Hello! I grew up and live in Oregon. The silver lining of a raincloud usually means a break in the rain, just enough time to walk the dog or take out the trash. "Hey!" the silver lining says. "I'm giving you a break! Stop and take advantage of it!" But maybe you're deep into your walk when the next cloud arrives, bringing more rain. And you get soaked. Neat.

Then again, maybe the idea of a silver lining is comforting to you. If so, awesome! But what if the silver lining is not the gift of the cloud? What if the gift of the cloud is the cloud itself?

I like clouds. They come in deep, mottled shades of gray: iron, black, dim white, even indigo. They promise a break from heat and provide moisture, often when it's badly needed. In the past few years, forest fires have ravaged the landscape I've both loved and taken for granted. August used to be a time of joy, a brief dry and warm respite from the long, dark, and damp of Pacific Northwest winter and spring. But the Augusts of recent years have brought smoke, intense heat, and fear. Our rain clouds, which used to arrive in September, now trickle in by October. When they finally arrive, they deliver blessed relief, their rains quenching the fires and soaking the forest floors, offering hope for a gentler fire season next year.

But these clouds also bring seasonal affective disorder. The lack of sunlight for months at a time permeates the region with an epidemic of depression. Long, rainy winters encourage people to cocoon, minimizing social interactions and time outdoors, creating a cycle of sadness and lethargy until the clouds lift again in the summer.

There are good things about clouds. There are tough things about clouds. Maybe clouds really are a strong metaphor for grief. But forget the silver lining. If the gift of the cloud is not the lining but the cloud itself, could it be that grief doesn't provide gifts via a lining at the edge, but may be the gift in and of itself?

What in the World Is Good about Grief?

I promise: this section avoids the clichés you already know and don't need to hear, e.g., "What doesn't kill us makes us stronger," "Loss makes us appreciate what we have," "Grief is a sign of having loved..." Forget all of that. Many of those corny sentiments aren't true anyway. Sure, something didn't kill us, but it certainly may have weakened us. Even if it did strengthen us, is strength truly better than loss? What if we are perfectly capable of appreciating and loving things in our lives without losing them? Still, the journey of grief—and the journey as a grieving Witch in particular—provides some surprising gifts.

The months after my last relationship ended were scarlet with rage; my fury at the person leaving me was a thick buffer for the heartbreak. I'd never known such rage before. I didn't know I was even capable of being that angry. The depth of the rage honestly scared me. It also humbled me. Many things about the relationship were wrong, and many close to me knew that. I had many kind, compassionate friends, whom I'd shut out of my life because they didn't approve of the relationship, welcome me back with sympathetic, open arms—a particularly humbling experience. Their love broke down intense, egotistical walls I'd built around myself and made me face truths I hadn't wanted to see. While I'd once believed my ex and I had a rare, cosmic, destined type of love, our poorly matched situation turned out to be not so special after all. My ex and I weren't special. *I* wasn't special. I was simply another woman who had found herself in an ill-fated romantic situation that hurt a lot of people—myself included.

Of course, I met my husband a few months later. It would be easy to say that the gift of losing my last relationship was that it made space for the right one, but the story is not so simple. That heartbreak came at the end of a long series of (nearly humorously) ill-fitted relationships. I had unconsciously accepted a personal story that I was destined to always be disappointed by love. But in the aftermath of the breakup, I stopped blaming the people I'd chosen to love and started looking at the choices that led me into such situations.

I often tell my husband that I'm glad I met him when I did. I truly believe that if I had met him before my heart was broken, our relationship would not have worked. It wasn't the ending of the last relationship that brought me the right love. The gift in that loss came from the opportunity to look at myself and make conscious changes, laying the groundwork for the right love to succeed. Simply saying, "Everything happens for a reason," meaning that I was meant to lose one love to find another, discards the hard work I did on myself. It also cheapens the gifts I found in my grief.

Loss Doesn't Offer Consolation Prizes

I first moved to Oregon when I was six. It was the mid-1980s, just a few years after Mount St. Helens had erupted, but piles of ash from the eruption remained alongside the highways with no place to go. Later, gorgeous glass paperweights made from the piles of displaced ash appeared in gift shops. At some point, my parents bought one and set it on a light, which glowed and gave the living room a dash of magick made from destruction.

The eruption of a volcano is a natural phenomenon. This is how the earth releases pressure. It's not an intentional act on the part the earth. The mountain didn't erupt in order to teach anything to the people whose homes it destroyed or lives it took with its rivers of ash. It was simply being a volcano. But some people who experienced the national disaster made art from its aftermath. The nation built a monument two years later, hosted by geologists and park rangers, who now offer knowledge and information about volcanoes. Did the mountain *have* to burst in order for people to make art or learn science? No. Did people have to make art or learn science *because* the mountain burst? Also no ... but they did. The aftermath of the loss created opportunity. Many people took advantage of that opportunity, and many beautiful things happened.

One important note regarding the ash from Mount St. Helens: The art mentioned above was created by people who collected ash from their yards, rooftops, or public areas when it was still abundant immediately after the eruption. Ash can still be found at the monument and in the area surrounding the volcano, but it is vital that visitors to the area *not* take ash, as it is a crucial part of the area's ecosystem and necessary for the land's regeneration. If you visit the monument or region around the volcano, leave the ash alone.

Journaling Prompt: What Grows in the New Space?

You've lost something or someone—what can grow in the space they left behind? If you've left a relationship, is there music you can listen to that your ex hated without their complaints? If you've lost a friend, is there time to do new things that they were never interested in doing, such as a hiking club or a trivia team? In the wake of losing a loved one to death, do you find yourself drawn to their hobbies or passions? Maybe you have a talent you've never explored because it seemed to be more "their thing"? Write a list, long or short. Consider setting a timer, and keep listing things until that timer goes off.

You don't have to pretend that what you've gained is better than what you've lost. Someday you may see it that way, but it's also possible that you will never see it that way. You don't have to. But since there is this opportunity, what can you do with it? Don't criticize yourself for finding a bit of joy in the opportunities provided by grief. This doesn't mean you didn't love who or what you lost. It's also fine if you find that the opportunities don't excite you. This is not about finding joy if there is no joy to be found. You are simply finding use for the rain and ash.

Hey! Look at Us Still Doing Our Thing!

Some losses can provide incredible courage. Now, this isn't an all-purpose model. If your loss came through a traumatic event, there may be serious new fears in its wake depending on how the loss transpired. If you lost someone to a car accident, driving may not feel good for a long time, if ever … but at the same time, you may suddenly feel brave enough to submit that dust-collecting novel to agents. What is the pain of rejection compared to the pain of your loss?

Another gift of the grief of my last relationship was that I no longer feared heartbreak. In previous relationships, I feared truly loving, as I feared that if my heart was broken, my life would be over. But when I did have my heart broken, my life continued. I continued breathing. Walking. Eating. Laughing. I deepened my pursuit of Witchcraft. I'd survived heartbreak. And because I was no longer afraid of it, I had the courage to open my heart to the true love of my life … and marry him.

We will never know what we're made of until we face grief. This is not fetishizing resiliency, which is its own tactic attempting to dismiss grief. But through grief, we can discover new things about ourselves, including a deeper understanding of who we are and what we want.

The Gifts in Separating from Community

Chances are, in your Witchcraft journey, you may find a community and eventually separate from it. Prior to the pandemic, this often happened when disagreements or logistical challenges broke down communities. The Witchcraft community is full of overworked, emotionally injured people, and while we are not a monolith, it is common for people to come to Witchcraft after experiencing trauma in a previous community or family. We are a collection of the outcast, bizarre, and strange. There are many blessings in that, and frankly, it's the company I prefer to keep. Unfortunately, it can also create situations where the unhealed parts of ourselves bump into one another. People frequently come to Witchcraft communities with unrealistic expectations of what they can do for them, such as being the family they never had, being a space to heal every wound they've ever experienced, or providing only positive and affirming experiences with all community members. Likewise, Witchcraft communities often try to be all things to all the people within them: family, therapy, spiritual guides, even resource centers for food and clothing. While these are noble goals, rarely does any community, spiritual or not, have the infrastructure or training to fit every need. Overpromising and under-delivering is extremely common in the Witchcraft world. This leads to burned-out people, disappointment, and resentment. Communities suffer, and sometimes fall apart altogether.

Even well-functioning communities don't fit everyone. There may be clashing lifestyles, personal beliefs, or personalities. While this is natural to every sort of community, it can be profoundly disappointing to people who crave connection with like-minded people. The pandemic shifted Witchcraft communities even further apart, as many of our beloved festivals, gatherings, and other events were terminated. Many have returned, but not all.

Whether by choice or circumstance, there is a good chance that at least once in our Witchcraft journey, we will lose the community we once loved. It may happen gently and leave warm memories and connections. Or it may happen dramatically with tension and hurt feelings. Either way, it's painful.

I left my Witchcraft community willingly. I was tired. To say I'd worked hard for the community is a gross understatement. For a time, it was my life. It held priority over work, health, and more. I thoroughly burned myself out. My departure received mixed responses. Some were supportive and understanding; others were scared and felt abandoned. A few were angry. I didn't leave angry, but at first, I was relieved, enjoying the time I'd found for myself and my husband, but grief eventually found me. I missed having the purpose, but I also grieved the time I'd given the community. How many more books could I have written if I hadn't spent so many evenings planning rituals? Where could I have traveled if I hadn't spent all that time organizing events and shuttling people to festivals? Would I have saved enough money to retire a little earlier if I hadn't poured so much into community expenses? When people tried to show me how much good I'd done, I often responded with an embittered, "So? What do I have to show for it?" It took a while, but the gifts of that grief eventually revealed themselves. I now have a clearer idea of my limits and gifts. The work I'd performed left me with concrete tools to create new creative and fulfilling projects that I can approach with a reasonable understanding of my abilities.

For many, the loss of a community may bloom into a gift of finding the "right" community. If that's the case for you, wonderful! But again, the gift may not be so simple as that. Your gift may include a deeper understanding of yourself and your needs, gifts that will serve you wherever you go and whatever you do.

Grief may come from tragedy and pain, but grief itself is not only made of tragedy and pain.

Where Are These Gifts?

Early in the grief journey, it may be tempting to look for the gifts because, as with the search for closure, we want our loss to have a purpose. But as with closure, these gifts are difficult to find in the early days. For one, it may be too painful to think of there being even a single gift in the loss. Even later in the journey, searching outright for these gifts also risks replicating the problematic model of grief being a problem to solve instead of a natural human experience that must simply be felt.

A Ritual to Embrace the Gifts of Grief

In time, the gifts of grief will appear. Sometimes, they appear and flow so naturally into your life that you won't even notice them until looking back in retrospect.

Suggested items: Paper or a canvas and writing or drawing implements (pens, paints, etc.)

Suggested incenses: Lavender, cedar, rosemary

The practice: Write a thank-you letter to the experience, detailing the things you appreciate about your life on this side of loss. List specific details. You may find it easier to paint or draw the things you appreciate as opposed to writing about them. This is fine too.

When you are finished with your piece, offer a prayer of gratitude over it. A suggested one is below:

> *I give thanks for what is lost, for what it has taken away,*
> *for the space remaining, for the potential for new*
> *things to find their way home.*
> *I offer thanks to those who have lost before me, may they*
> *guide me and bless me with the gifts.*

For the gifts I do not see, I offer thanks to them and know
  I will see in time.
A slice of my tears for a breath of clean air,
May fire burn clear, may the waves run strong,
Let the gifts flow freely and may my heart wrap them as
  their own.

Discovering the Gifts of Grief Is Its Own Journey

This is not a target mark to hit. It is not a task to complete. Every loss has a gift encoded in it, but it's not the task of the griever to find it, at least initially. If you can't see the gift in your grief, it's simply not time. When you are ready, the gift will reveal itself. It's quite possible you are enjoying that gift right now without being aware of it.

An Exercise for Being the You Now That You Needed Then

This exercise is best completed when at least three months' time has passed since your loss.

Imagine sitting with yourself in the moments after your loss. See your grieving face: acknowledge its pain, fury, despair, confusion, numbness. What would you tell yourself then about what is happening now? Comfort that past self. Know that the act of comforting yourself in that time also comforts you in this time. Create a story. Write a letter. Paint. Draw. Make music. Go outside and speak to the trees. Many years ago, I spoke to past me at a lake on a full moon night. Do what you need to do to communicate with your past self, the one fresh to the loss. My example is below:

"Hey. You. Me. People aren't trash. Love isn't fake, but it hurts people sometimes, and this time, you got hurt. However, the greatest gift that man could have given you was walking away. He broke a pattern that day. He set you free. Listen, there will be days, months, and years of rage ahead of you, followed by guilt, and eventually mourning not for the lover who vanished but the friend you lost. It was a great and bitter price, but this loss is giving you new eyes to show you where mistakes were made and which patterns should be shattered. It will give you clarity on what you think you want, and finally, the love you actually want. Now, you think your path is tarnished, but it wasn't even real to begin with. Your real path is ahead of you. Soon, you'll long to thank that man for breaking your heart. Yes, it is *an* end. But it's not *the* end. Now that you know you can survive heartbreak, you won't fear it as you once did."

An Exercise for Connecting with the Future You That You Need Now

There is a future you who, while still carrying your loss within them, and their life is shaped by the loss you've experienced. While this can mean Future You will have some challenges rooted in your loss, there will also be blessings and strengths rooted in it as well. Exploring the possibilities of those blessings and strengths can help place your current loss in a productive context.

Once you've completed communicating to your past self, whether that is through writing a letter, making a piece of art, or simply speaking to a vision of yourself in meditation, take a moment and envision your future self. What might your life look like ten, twenty, thirty years from now? How is it shaped by the loss you've experienced? What gifts does future you appreciate?

Be creative in how you speak to future you. If you sang to past you, maybe write to future you. If you feel called to paint or draw, let future you take the lead and dictate the image. Don't be constrained in any part of this exercise because you don't think you're good at a certain thing (writing, drawing, etc.). No one will see this unless you let them.

Here is my letter to my future self:

> "I write this a year after losing the baby. The loss still haunts me, and I'm sure that it haunts you occasionally too. But I believe it has given you more appreciation for the life you are now living. It's made you both more patient and more resilient. You don't fear setting boundaries on your time because you've learned its value. In a strange way, it taught you that you don't owe the world your exhaustion. You know you don't need to work so hard just to justify your existence. I hope that you no longer fear loss, but if you do still fear it, that you have confidence to navigate it."

An Exercise for Bringing Your Yous Together

If you'd like, take this work one step further and sit with both selves—the past and the future.

Imagine for a moment that past you and future you are stopping by for coffee or tea. Use whatever method best creates the experience for you: meditation and visualization, writing it as a story, singing or playing a song for each, drawing a picture, etc. Maybe even make three cups of coffee or tea—one for you and one for each of them! Explore how past you might react to where and how you are living now. How is past you impressed, confused, or even disappointed? Do the same for future you. What does future you recognize as important? What would future you tell you to ignore or disregard? If you struggle to hear or imagine what past or future you might say, don't force it. It may come later in a dream or realization while awake. Taking a gentle approach with this exercise will yield the best results.

After giving your past and future selves the chance to share their thoughts, feelings, and opinions on your life at present, take the time to show them both how your loss nurtured opportunities in your life. Perhaps your last partner was allergic to cats and so you couldn't have one, but now that they're gone, you have a cat and it's the love of your life. Imagine how past you, perhaps mourning the loss of the partner, would react when they see your beloved feline. Next, turn to future you and share what you hope to do with the opportunities your loss has given you. Maybe you are currently mourning the friends and parts of the life you had before you embraced a sober path … but with the money you're saving by not purchasing alcohol or other substances and the increased focus and clarity you have, you're planning to purchase a home for future you.

Take a moment to thank past you for weathering the past loss, which has provided the gifts and opportunities you have now. Then, take a moment and let future you thank you for creating the opportunities to better their life, opportunities rooted in the loss or losses you've navigated.

Gratitude for the Gifts of Grief Will Ebb and Flow

There will be days when you appreciate what you've gained, and days when those gains feel like nothing at all. On the days that you don't feel good about what you've gained, it doesn't mean that those gifts were not real. They were real then. They may be real again. Grief is a fluid beast, constantly shifting with the tides of time. Allow it to do that. Even if the gifts were only there for a day, gifts they still were.

More gifts will follow.

8

Casting the New Spell

At the end of summer 2020 (Labor Day weekend for those living in the States), the area where I live suffered. It happened fast. My husband and I went to my parents' house for a socially distanced picnic in their backyard. The air carried a faint hint of smoke, which is not unusual for early autumn in our part of the world, where many farmers have autumnal burning practices. But the winds were unusually high, and when we arrived at my parents' suburban home, the smoke was strong. By that evening, the sky across most of the state was a scorching Halloween orange, something I'd only seen in apocalyptic nightmares. Even our dog refused to go outside. Rare, high-force winds had knocked down powerlines at the end of a brutal dry season, inciting massive forest fires around the state.

It was nothing I experienced growing up in Oregon. Climate change has made our summers hotter and drier, and a century of fire suppression and prevention of Indigenous selective burning practices has packed the beautiful green forests with the kindling equivalent to a garage packed with newspaper and cardboard boxes with a spewing furnace in the middle. The forests, which have held the heart and soul of this region since the first people came here nearly thirty thousand years ago, were aflame. Many of us didn't know if we would need to evacuate or if we were safe to stay, and few of us knew where we could safely go. It all depended on where the winds blew.

In the week that followed, I prepared a "to-go" tote, something that my Californian relatives had done for years but something new to me. I didn't have time to grieve over the glimpse of the new world I may be living in, where such fires are a threat. I could only think about what was most important to take: marriage certificate, passports, medications, my grandmother's cookbook, pet supplies, the totes of journals I'd kept since I was a child. I'd not seen the sun in days, as it was eclipsed by the orange sky, reflecting the fires not only taking out forests, but homes and lives as well. The smoky air smelled of burning rubber and hot metal. I tried not to think of what remnants I might be inhaling when I'd have to open the front door. While I was pacing the house, deciding what to bring with me, I passed one of our many altars. I looked at the statues, the offerings, the trinkets—things that I once thought invaluable to my Witchcraft practice.

"I won't bring any of it with me," I said to the altar. It was not an apology but a statement. "I can rebuild all of this."

Luckily, we did not have to evacuate. Eventually, I felt comfortable enough to return treasured possessions to their storage spaces. But the air was still so thick with gray and brown smoke that we could not see across the street. Oregon, long known for its clean air, had the worst air quality in the world for weeks after the fires began. Laying on my couch in my house, I could not take a full breath. It was then my grief began.

This was not the Oregon I knew growing up, and it was not the Oregon I had promised my husband when we moved here. In a state roughly the size of the United Kingdom, there was no clean air to be found. Traveling to a place where the air was cleaner would have meant a two-day drive. There was a part of me that did not want to believe it, that wanted to believe this was an anomaly, a freak thing that would never happen again. I fought the grief creeping in—that for the world I'd known once before climate change, and for the approach of the world I'd been warned about in our science classes as a child, the one I didn't want to believe would ever happen. Surely, they'd find a "cure" for climate change before it would be a problem, right? Or the issues would happen long after I was dead and gone? No. As it turned out, that horrifying new world was here.

Grief Changes Us

We are not the same people on the other side of grief as we were before.

Sometimes the changes are small, but other times, we hardly recognize ourselves on the other side. Grief changes us as Witches too. It may have been the tenth day of unbreathable air when I looked at my altar and realized it wasn't mine anymore.

I'd built it myself when I was living alone and tended it nightly, and made years of magick there. When my husband and I married, we started a "joint" altar, and I visited my old altar less. But it took the destruction of the land around me to realize that I'd lost connection to the old altar and most of the permanent items on it. I took it apart and offered it to the teenaged daughter of a friend who had recently come into her own as a Witch. I then went to the altar my husband and I shared and removed everything that once had meaning for me, leaving the items belonging to my husband. I returned objects that still carried some connection for me, but found that few of them did.

The fire and smoke reminded me of the foundational truth that everything I needed as a Witch was within me. Altars and magickal objects were replaceable. If I needed to sacrifice them in exchange for mine and my family's lives, I would do it.

I had some guilt, wondering if I was abandoning the gods I'd so carefully worshipped for so long or even myself as a Witch, but it passed. When we're facing the sheer power and fury of our planet, we connect with our most ancient ancestors, who were so steeped in fear of and reverence for their environment that they built whole religions and traditions to appease it.

I was no longer a Witch who needed an altar. I was a Witch who needed to keep breathing.

How Grief Changes Magick

Grief changes magick because grief changes us. If magick is the practice of ritually changing the world to suit our desires, those desires will change after loss. As climate change continues, our collective wishes as Witches will also change. When I first came into Witchcraft, the goal of many Witches was "love and light and peace." Many Witches used magick to increase prosperity, love, or otherwise, but generally kept to gentle, personal outcomes. Indeed, many Witches today still pursue those same magickal goals, which are perfectly valid, but the scope has grown. Witches around the world use magick to combat tyranny and cast spells for justice as much as peace. Witches are using magick not just to heal the natural world. They are using it to wake up those with the greatest power to influence this global crisis before it's too late.

Your standard practice of magick may suit you beautifully in the immediate days after your loss, but for many, grief changes their approach to magick. You may find yourself drawn to new deities, traditions, or paths. Sometimes, grief and loss can empower latent magickal abilities, whether they be ones long unused or ones you never knew you had. But for many, embracing a new path or powers will come in time.

A Ritual for Embracing the New Witch Within

Leave your altar. Set aside your tools, robes, etc. Strip your magick down to basics.

Take yourself to the place, or a similar one, where you first realized you were a Witch. For me, that was outside looking at the moon. If that landscape is too different from the one where you currently reside, create a comparable space. For example, if your place was by the ocean and you now live in a landlocked place, play the sounds of the ocean on your phone or computer. Try to remember the feelings you had when you first realized you were a Witch. As best as you are able, recall what was happening in your life at the time: any wonder, fear, confusion, or joy embedded in that time.

Bless this time. Then, allow it to fade. If need be, consider bidding it farewell.

Now, reflect on your current needs. Acknowledge any anger, fear, sorrow, joy, etc. without judging or analyzing it. Envision yourself in your full Witch form, whatever that may be. Perhaps you see yourself in swirling robes or running barefoot through a forest. Maybe you see yourself floating on a cloud above. Or maybe you even see yourself as a swirl of brightly colored energy. Maybe you just see yourself in your regular clothes. All are fine, and remember, this is only for this moment. It's not meant to shape your identity as a Witch for all time.

Acknowledge where you have sustained injury as a Witch, whether through the loss you've just experienced or simply as a human walking a human path. Ask the injured Witch within you what they need right now. Is it to be near nature? To build a new altar? To change paths? Or even stop practicing Witchcraft altogether for a while? Sit with that Witch for as long as you are able. If you do not get an answer immediately, don't despair. Often, the answers we seek will come later through dreams, moments of synchronicity, or messages from trusted friends or other co-conspirators.

Don't judge or try to reason with the inner Witch. Follow their lead for what kind of Witchcraft they need right now. Know that this new way of approaching your Witchcraft may only be temporary and you will likely return to the way you practiced before. Then again, grief may have opened an entirely new magickal path for you and it's only the beginning.

Take this next journey moment to moment.

If You're Stuck

If you are feeling the need to practice Witchcraft but are not getting answers or visions from your inner Witch, here is a practice you can utilize until a path more unique to you unfolds.

Select a time each day. The time is up to you. It can be in the morning with your coffee or tea, in the afternoon, in the evening before bedtime, or even in the middle of the night. If you are physically able to do so, go outside. If you have physical or other restrictions that prevent you from going outside, sitting or standing by an open window is perfectly fine. Be mindful of your safety. If the time that works best for you is midnight but you live in a place where it is not safe to go outdoors at midnight, use the open window practice.

However it is feasible for you to do so, make an offering to the spirits of the land where you live. Keep this simple and as environmentally sensitive as possible. Even if now in your grief journey you are struggling to believe in a spirit world, try to remember that there is a living pulse within all things, and to this you can give reverence and recognition. Good offering suggestions might be water, birdseed appropriate to the birds of your region, collecting trash, singing a song, offering a prayer, or whatever calls to you.

You can do this in the city as well! I lived in New York City for thirteen years and often snuck offerings into parks or left them at the bases of sidewalk trees. Again, the offering need not be physical. Prayers, songs, even a deep, cleansing breath and acknowledgment of the earth around you is a fine offering.

Commit to doing this every day for thirty days. To stay with this work, be creative in how you do it. Maybe you do it while on your way to work, such as during the walk to the bus or through your open car window. Maybe you do it while walking your dog. If you're lucky enough to have an outdoor space adjacent to your home, step outside in the morning while you're waiting for your coffee to brew or kettle to boil. If your health and physical ability allows, do it despite bad weather. A quick step into hard rain, snow, cold, or even heat can do wonders for connecting to the magick of this world. Naturally, be mindful of your physical safety. If you're sick, stay inside. If there's a hurricane or tornado, stay inside.

If there's an air quality advisory, stay inside. Magick thrives when the practitioner is creative with restrictions. Be creative.

As time goes on, you'll likely find yourself adding more things to your magickal routine. Maybe you pull a tarot card after your offering. Maybe you start including a prayer of thanks at night (even if you're not entirely sure who you're thanking or what you're thanking them for). Go back to basics. Honoring the planet and the spirits that surround you is a powerful way to connect with your new Witch self.

A Practice for Looping In Your Ancestors

For better or worse, working with ancestors is a building block of a Witchcraft practice. The good news is that it's relatively easy to do, no matter your background. The challenge is that ancestor veneration is sometimes a fraught process. Many of us don't know our ancestors, or we know very few of them. If we've been mistreated or ostracized by our families of origin, the idea of connecting with ancestors can be scary or painful. We may have some problematic ancestors, whom we want nothing to do with. However, not every single ancestor need be venerated. Each of us comes from thousands of people. Not all of them were great people. But some were.

Not all ancestors need to be related to you by blood either. If you were adopted, the ancestors in your adopted family are every bit as valid and supportive of you as those of blood. If you connect with artists or historical figures who inspire you, those ancestors may be present for you as well.

A beginning step in venerating your ancestors is to pray for the peace of those who lived and died well. If you have space and desire, set up an ancestor shrine or altar with photos of ancestors you loved. If you did not know your ancestors or do not want to connect with the ones you did know, suggested items for the altar might be effigies of deities that are known for opening the gates to other worlds, e.g., St. Peter, Anubis, Hekate, etc. Leave a hospitable offering, such as a cup of hot coffee or tea. If you're comfortable offering alcohol, whiskey, rum, or wine work as well.

If your ancestors said prayers that you also know and feel comfortable with saying, consider offering that prayer for them. For me, it's "The Lord's Prayer," both the Catholic and Protestant versions, as I had ancestors devout to both traditions. However, saying this prayer has been a journey for me. When I was a child, it scared me, as I was afraid of summoning God and being destroyed for my sins. As a young Witch, I feared it would offend the new gods I had embraced. Now, I see it as something comforting to the ancestors, both those I knew and didn't know, and I use it as a common language with them when I want to offer them peace. If you do not have knowledge of or desire to use such a prayer, feel free to create your own. Here is one you can also use, if you'd like:

> *Ancestors dear, of blood and of love,*
> *For those who lived in goodness and passed in tears of others,*
> *May you be at peace, may you be held in light.*
> *May your regrets be banished, and may your dreams continue through those who live now.*

Conclude with your preferred ending, e.g., "So mote it be," "Ashe," "Amen," etc.

The goal of this work is to offer peace and elevation to ancestors who lived and died well. The idea of dying well can be a challenge to envision, as many people who lived good lives of integrity may have died in traumatic ways (accidents, childbirth, war, etc.). But it's not the method of dying that determines a good death, but rather how others around them received it. If they lived well and were good to others in their life, they would have been mourned. Their passing would have caused sorrow to those who knew them; it would not have been a relief. This is the story of a good death.

Doing rites for the peace and elevation of ancestors who lived and died well is a gentle, comforting practice that can help you ease your way back into a Witchcraft path or carve out a new one.

A Ritual to Take Ancestral Work a Step Further When You Are Ready

Ancestors are relatable because they suffered. In prior centuries, when diseases were much quicker to kill and the world was generally more violent, ancestors were quite used to loss. Even if they were unusually lucky and spared from most suffering, they were human. Therefore, they suffered the passing of loved ones, heartbreak, the severing of friendships, or the loss of a homeland. Ancestors understand loss.

After losing our baby, I prayed at my ancestor shrine often, calling for assistance from those who had lost children. Although I was not aware of any specific ancestors who lost children, whether through illness, accident, miscarriage, or stillbirth, it's a common enough occurrence (particularly in previous generations) that some-one along the line had surely experienced a similar loss. I prayed to whoever that might be to help me get through this time. In this space, where I did not know who I might be speaking to and therefore could not anticipate responses or judgments, I could lean fully into my grief process.

Remember, you come from thousands of lives that contained love, loss, heartbreak, environmental destruction, displacement, separation, and more. You do not need to know specific stories to know they existed. Having been alive at one time is enough. If you happen to know of a specific ancestor whose experience mirrored your loss, you can certainly contact them by either going to their place of burial (if you are able) or placing a picture in a space you have dedicated to your ancestors.

Be mindful that not all ancestors want to be called upon for magickal work. Some of them are working on their own healing process. Some need rest. Others may not be particularly sympathetic to your plight, as they may not have been particularly sympathetic people in life. However, many will be ready and available to you. Developing a relationship with ancestors also involves trial and error. They were and still are people, and people are naturally flawed. Some people turn up better for us in our time of grief than others. Ancestors are no different.

If you cannot think of a specific person, asking for help from an anonymous ancestor who lived well and is sympathetic to your situation is a good plan. This ancestor will make their way to you.

Consider designating a specific candle to helpful ancestors. When you light it, it will be a sign that you need to speak with a sympathetic someone on the other side.

Make a kind but feasible offering and perform a "ritual signal" to let the ancestors know you are ready to connect with them (such as saying a specific prayer, lighting a candle, both, or something else). Then, speak to what you need. As always, using your own words is quite powerful. If you do not have your own words, you can use the following. Feel free to edit to suit your purposes:

> *Beyond the veil, beyond the grave,*
> *Love remains, and breath reclaim,*
> *I hold a great burden, I ask for help now,*
> *To direct me, to guide me, to hold me when I cry.*

You may wish to explain your situation. If it is too hard to put it into words, never fear. Your ancestors will recognize the situation, and even if they don't, they will recognize your pain.

To offer thanks, say a prayer or incantation for their peace, without any further requests for a time.

You may feel a response from the ancestors immediately. You may receive clear guidance later, through dreams or other powerful moments. You may not receive anything concrete at all. But know that they are there. Ythat you are not walking alone in this situation.

A Ritual for "Being Here Now"

When I was leading my coven, we called in the elemental guardians of the different quarters, as many Wiccan-influenced groups do. We ended the call with "Be here now." I used this too because my coveners strongly identified with it, but it always seemed strange that we would command elemental forces to "be" with us when they were so much bigger than we and already present through the rain, the sun, the wind, and the soil. But one day, it occurred to me that perhaps we weren't specifically summoning these beings with "be here now" so much as we were inadvertently telling ourselves to be present, to be aware of the beings that were already with us. We were the ones we were summoning to "be here now."

The phrase meant a lot to me as I was returning to Witchcraft after my loss. It was more than commanding spirits or beings to be with me, but rather reminding myself to be present with not just the magick around me but also myself as a Witch. The practice of "being here now" helped me to recognize exactly where I was in both my Witchcraft and grief journeys at that moment and honor that without looking to the past or the future, or thinking of who or what I "should" be.

When you are ready to practice Witchcraft again, here is a suggested ritual to help you reorient yourself with your new magick in this part of your grief journey:

Using a compass (most of us have compass apps on our phones), turn to the east. Doing this outside is recommended, but inside is fine if that's what's accessible. Focus on the air around you: the air you breathe, the way air touches your skin. Talk to yourself in this moment. You are not summoning the elemental beings so much as the part of yourself that connects with these forces.

In North America, many people associate air with the east, fire with the south, water with the west, and earth with the north. However, this can be constructed differently depending on your location and viewpoint. When I lived in New York, my coven invoked water in the east, as the Atlantic Ocean was to the east of us, and air in the west, acknowledging the jet stream that brought wind and many weather patterns to the city. Take the time to think about what makes the most sense for your own understanding and your region, as this is a powerful step in being here now.

The following ritual is written using the associations of air/east, fire/south, water/west, and earth/north. Feel free to rearrange the associations or order based on your traditions, training, or understanding.

While facing the east, if you are indoors, consider opening a window or facing a running box fan. If you are outside, even better! Invoke the air part of self with any invocation you choose. If you are uncertain of what to say, here is an invocation you can use:

> *Witch within me of breath and sigh,*
> *of breeze and wind,*
> *of gust and squall,*
> *Be here, be here, be here now.*

After saying the words, notice how your body reacts to air. Breathe as deeply as possible. How does the air feel in your lungs? Now, notice how your spirit reacts to the air. What senses or emotions do you feel, if any? Does air bring you peace or anxiety? Is there a sense of freedom or perhaps fear? Don't judge or analyze your experience or lack thereof. This is simply about bringing yourself as the Witch, as you are, into this present moment.

Next, turn to the south. Consider lighting a candle or, if you are outdoors, a small, contained fire. Carefully interact with the flame. Watch it dance or place your hands nearby to feel its warmth. Connect with the spirit of fire by saying the following or a different invocation of your own choosing or creation:

Witch within me of flame and embers,
Heat and fervor,
Fever and burns,
Be here, be here, be here now!

As you did with air, notice how the fire affects your body and spirit. How does the space around the fire feel when close to your skin? Again, keep a safe distance from the fire so you do not cause injury to yourself. But within this safe distance, how does your body feel? Are you warmed in a comforting way or feeling discomfort from too much warmth? How does your spirit react to the fire? Are you energized? Overwhelmed? Do you feel fortified or maybe even impassioned? Does the fire incite an internal fury? Again, don't judge or analyze your experience or lack thereof. Just bring yourself as the Witch, as you are, into this present moment.

Now, turn to the west. If you have a natural body of water to the west of you, such as a creek, lake, or the ocean, feel free to utilize it if it's safe to do so. If you do not have access to a natural body of water or would simply prefer to do this work indoors, you can use a bowl of water or a full bathtub. Connect with the spirit of water by saying the following or a different invocation of your own choosing or creation:

Witch within me of ocean and rain,
Of tears and sweat,
Mists and storm,
Be here, be here, be here now!

Anoint yourself with the water, and again, notice how it affects your body as well as your spirit. Is the water refreshing or chilling? Does it feel cleansing and peaceful or cold and unkind? How does your spirit react to the water? Is there a sense of release? Or perhaps a feeling of being exposed? Do you feel calmer or possibly vulnerable? Does water connect with any tears that still need shedding? Remember, don't judge or analyze your experience or lack thereof. Just bring yourself as the Witch, as you are, into this present moment.

Finally, turn to the north. If you are outside and it's accessible for you to do so, you can crouch with your hands in the soil or even lay on the ground to connect with earth. If it's preferable or more feasible to do this work indoors, hold a beloved rock or crystal. Connect with the spirit of earth by saying the following or a different invocation of your own choosing or creation:

> *Witch within me of soil and stone,*
> *Of rocks and gem,*
> *Dust and bone,*
> *Be here, be here, be here now.*

If your hands are in the soil, anoint your forehead and heart with it. If you are using a crystal, rock, or stone, touch it to your forehead and heart. Notice how this piece of earth affects your body and spirit. Is it grounding or cold? Does it feel fortifying or desolate? How does your spirit react to the earth? Is there a feeling of being supported or possibly abandoned? Do you feel grounded? Weighed down? Does earth help you feel more connected to the living world or painfully insignificant? Perhaps you feel something completely different. Don't judge or analyze your experience or lack thereof.

Just bring yourself as the Witch, as you are, into this present moment.

Now, stand in the middle of the four places. Embrace the title of *Witch* in a way that feels correct in this present moment. That may include humming, swaying, cackling, or simply saying aloud, "I am a Witch."

Loss often separates people from long-practiced religious or spiritual traditions. If this is your experience and you find yourself struggling to connect with your previous Witchcraft practice or tradition, it may be helpful to take this time and remember that you are still a Witch. Your beliefs in Witchcraft will change and shift, and nothing is likely to change them more than grief. Remember to recognize where you've been, how you feel, what is present for you.

It's possible that it may take time for you to fully feel like a Witch again. Then again, for many people, grief makes them feel like super-Witches. Maybe you'll feel something in between or something else altogether. Whatever your experience may be, take this journey a day at a time. When a day is too long, take it a moment at a time. In time, your new way of Witching will become part of you, perhaps even more so than the way you felt as a Witch before.

Grief Changes Us, but It Does Not Define Us.

Prior to the grief journey, both for our child and for the forests after the fires, my Witchcraft was highly deity-centered with an occasional nod toward the ancestors and earth. Now, my Witchcraft is far more firmly rooted in reverence for my ancestors and for the earth than before. There is a humility that comes with grief, a greater respect for those who have gone before. The earth becomes not simply a pretty place to walk but a living being with indiscriminate and sometimes punishing cycles. The reverence may go from, "Oh! How pretty you are … thank you for providing food and air" to "Thank you for all these things and also not killing me and my family." This humility can help us tap back into a far more ancient relationship with the earth, before modern inventions and contemporary agriculture lured us into thinking that the earth was a permanent provider. To our ancestors, the earth was a formidable place in which it might be possible to be a partner or maybe a supplicant, but it was not a kindly barista who would simply provide because it was asked nicely.

But then, things happen that remind us that this planet holds kindness and beauty.

A week and change after the smoke filled our state, after I thought it would never rain again, we experienced another unusual weather event. The skies opened and a deluge came down. Early September is typically quite dry in Oregon, and if there's any rain, it's usually gentle and misty. This was a torrent. The weather apps hadn't even predicted it. I stepped out on our porch barefoot and in my pajamas, and watched it pour and soak the earth. My tears fell, mingled with the fresh, wet air.

It was a different kind of rain. Each drop contained a prayer from someone, somewhere in the world—the magick from their own traditions sent to my region to heal our area. I believed in that magick more than I'd ever believed in magick before. The next day, I breathed clean air for the first time in two weeks. The sky was once again blue, not orange, black, gray, or brown. It was magick manifested in healing, fed by the belief and love of many I knew and many more whom I'd never meet. This is how our world has always used magick: fueled by a love for one another great enough to cause a change in the weather, even when it's never thought possible.

A Jagged Rite of Passage

I've left a few organizations. I saw a lot of people, decades older than me, who were not demonstrating wisdom, discernment, or boundaries. I liked a lot of them, but I had to separate. I also chose to withdraw from a very powerful witchcraft tradition simply because I couldn't give it justice anymore. And I had a lot of grief. About a year after I left, there were other key people who also left, and it just imploded really after that. Sometimes you leave for your own safety, emotional or psychic. Other times, you leave out of deep respect for the egregore of the group or the tradition. The grief was literal tears and emails of sadness, saying, "I can see that you're doing this for the right reasons...I wish that it was some other way." Sometimes the grief manifested in anxiety around how I could now navigate these tricky, lineage-based webs without disrespecting anyone or myself. Grief was a comforting container, like this sacred blanket or cloak, which gave meaning and texture to the whole thing. To me, grief is exceptionally sacred. It can be one witch going to another witch who has the strength and capacity to hold and hear your grief—which may manifest as rage, sadness and tears, or confusion and disorientation—and the other Witch having the ability to hear you and witness you. Of course, I, like any human, can get caught in ricochet bullshit. But I do a triple soul alignment or iron pentacle practice or recite the "Charge of the Goddess" and go into a semi-trance state and listen to whichever goddess wants to walk through in that moment. I call it *devotional ecstasy*. I go to one of my working altars inside, outside, or next to the ocean. And I sing and drum or recite the Charge. I go into this altered state where I allow myself to have that catharsis of sobbing or laughing, or then calling up a friend and being like, "May I vent to you?" Those rituals helped bring me into a more grounded, centered state. So much about witchcraft does that, right? Our tools ultimately ground, clarify, contain, distill. That's what magick does.

Sometimes, the grief (of losing community) is kind of jagged, because you still might be connected to some of those people. There might be the loss of rich, regular ritual. I think the grief can manifest as nostalgia, and for a lot of witches and Pagans, the grief manifests as rage. But if you engage the grief, it creates space for you. In the walking away, yes, there might be the jagged moments of resentment, but ultimately, these situations create space. One can still feel connected, in a beautiful way, to those times and to those people. But to someone who just walked away, I would say, "Yeah. That fucking sucks," but also, "Congratulations on getting out of there." Maybe there was actual abuse. Maybe there was transgression of boundaries. Maybe you outgrew it. Maybe the teachings that you held sacred were being treated like shit. Maybe you were ejected, or you needed to move on to stay in integrity with yourself. This may be one of the most powerful rites of passage and initiations you will ever know.

~Fio Gede Parma

9

Help for the Grieving

Many Witches are natural fixers, perhaps drawn to Witchcraft in the first place to control things that happen, not just for themselves but for the people they love. These same Witches are not afraid of getting their hands deep into the grief of others. I recall with both fondness and cringe the many public rituals I once led that became de facto grieving rituals. It surely had to do with my method of leaning more into emotion than magick in these rituals, which would often conclude with at least one person weeping into the arms of another. The people present were not afraid to, if permitted, embrace them and hold their grief.

Many Witches are not afraid of grief. Some may fear allowing the wounds to heal.

While Witches offer a lot of energy toward grieving people, our communities sometimes lack the infrastructure and practices to help grieving people with practical means. Sometimes, we go too far. After my first miscarriage, I blogged about our loss as a way of being "real" with people in our community, while also trying to destigmatize a sad but natural process. Unfortunately, things didn't go as planned. A few days later, I opened my Messenger inbox to see an unsolicited tarot reading about my loss from someone I barely knew. Being an avid tarot reader, I knew nasty cards when I saw them, and although the sender tried to put a positive spin on things, it didn't help. First of all, I hadn't wanted a tarot reading on it. Second, I was horrified by what I read. The well-intentioned action added a thick layer of doom and gloom to my already-painful situation.

Also, how was I to respond? Should I use my energy to try to educate this person on how *not* to assist a grieving person or just ignore it? Eventually, the person realized they'd overstepped and sent me an apology, at which point I was faced with another choice: accept the apology to make them feel better or use the opportunity to express how their actions had impacted me and risk looking like "the bad guy"? I eventually chose a middle ground, explaining that their action was hurtful even though I knew it came from a genuine desire to help.

This chapter felt important to write because, while everyone will eventually experience loss, there are some people who haven't experienced it yet. Alternatively, they may have experience with one kind of loss and might approach loss with a single-lens approach. How one person responds to the loss of a relationship will differ from how another responds to the loss of a beloved pet. There is no one-size approach to helping grieving people. Their feelings about their loss will differ depending on who they are and what kind of loss they have experienced. Loss is simple, but grief is complicated.

Ways to Help Grieving People

Naturally, we want to help the grieving people we love. But if our best intentions could potentially make things worse, what can we do? Below are a few ways to consider helping those you love when they are grieving.

Reach Out, but Not Too Much

A grieving person may not reach out to you. Grief can make picking up a phone or opening Messenger feel like a foreign language. But a grieving person who does not reach out may still want support. Particularly in the deepest throes of grief, they are also likely to feel quite isolated. The onus will be on the people in their lives to contact them. Call your grieving loved one. They may not pick up, and you might need to do the old-fashioned thing of leaving a voicemail. They'll listen when they're ready. Texting is also a true gift to the grieving process. It's generally less invasive, and seeing the words "Thinking of you" on the screen can be comforting. The grieving person may not respond, but they will know that someone out there is holding space for them. For many grieving people, this is deeply appreciated.

When I was in the thickest of my grief process over our child, an old friend asked if she could call, and we arranged a time, but when that time came, I did not have the energy to pick up the phone. Still, seeing her name on the screen was comforting. I felt guilty initially about not answering, but in the coming days, she texted me a picture of a bonfire she'd lit in her backyard with the caption, "This one is for you." She'd understood, and knowing a fire was burning for me three thousand miles away was a balm on my heart.

If the friend is nonresponsive, don't repeat the calls or texts too often. They may want space, and while they will likely appreciate knowing they are on your mind, too many calls can be intrusive, and it will be extra labor for them to explain that to you. If you are worried about a nonresponsive friend's welfare, consider contacting someone else who may be even closer to them, such as a spouse, immediate family member, roommate, or otherwise. If you believe your loved one may be in danger of harming themselves, seek professional intervention.

Don't Say, "Let Me Know If You Need Anything"

Again, this puts work on the grieving person. They may not even know what they need, and they are unlikely to take you up on your offer. Instead, make suggestions of things that might be helpful, such as: "Is there anyone you'd like for me to notify about your loss?" or "I'm going to the grocery store. What do you need that I can pick up?" or even, "Are there any annoying people you need me to help keep at bay?"

These offers are invaluable to a grieving person. When someone is grieving, everything is hard: grocery shopping, cooking, cleaning, caring for children or pets, work, etc. Do get permission from the grieving person or someone in their close vicinity first, but instead of saying, "Do you need help with anything?" offer something specific like, "A bunch of us would like to bring over a series of dinners for you. Would that be helpful? If so, is there anything in particular you'd like to eat?" If you have the financial ability to do so, sending gift cards for meal delivery services or housekeeping services can be very helpful. Even if the grieving person doesn't use them right away, it's a nice treat to lean into later when they are ready. My husband and I received a lot of meal delivery gift cards while we grieved. We didn't use them immediately, but later we combined them and ordered a big meal for a family gathering, which was great fun and created a wonderful memory.

If they say, "No, thank you," don't push it. Just by offering, you have shown you care. Continue showing you care by respecting a boundary when it is set.

Invite Them to Things

Before doing this, it can be a good idea to check in with a third-party person who is close to the grieving person and can be a good judge of whether the invitation would be welcome. For example, someone who is heartbroken over a divorce may not feel great about hearing about your engagement party. A person who is sorting through their possessions after a devastating house fire may not want to know about your housewarming potluck. If you're close enough to the grieving person, you could ask them directly how they might feel about being included on the invitation list. The care and consideration for the grieving person may well be appreciated. Some grieving people will appreciate the distraction and will welcome the invite, so don't blatantly leave them off your list.

Good events to share with grieving people include things that don't require a lot of personal interaction: a nice hike, live music, a fair or festival, etc. One-on-one or small-group interactions are often best for grieving people, although some grieving people may enjoy a raucous party. Just having the opportunity to be out and about can do a lot to break up the monotony in the days after a loss.

Don't be offended if they say no, or attend but go home early. Don't try to "pep them up" if they do come out but seem quiet, sad, or withdrawn. It can be helpful if you say, "Hey, I'm glad you're here, but if you want to take off, it's totally fine."

Listen—Even at Seemingly Random Times

A grieving person may not feel like talking at the precise moment you ask, "Would you like to talk about it?" They also may be tired of answering, "How are you?" A kind thing to say in the aftermath of their loss is, "I don't want to pry, but please know you can talk about this with me at any time."

Be prepared: the grieving person may choose to talk about their loss at a seemingly odd moment. When I moved to New York City in 2003, I met many people who were present at 9/11, but they didn't say much about it. However, as the ten-year anniversary of the tragic day approached, I was walking down the street with a friend when they suddenly stopped. We hadn't been talking about anything related to the event, but my friend suddenly described a horrific sight they'd witnessed on that fateful day. A similar thing happened with other friends and even strangers on the subway. With no impetus to discuss the event, they would create a strange connection, such as, "Hey, where did you get those shoes? Those are cool. But they're so different than the shoes I was wearing when the towers fell …" and a heartbreaking story would follow.

This may happen with your grieving friends. It may take you off guard. Do your best to listen without trying to solve or fix. Try not to remark on any seeming randomness, e.g., "Geez. Where did *that* come from?" Also, don't change the topic to "get their mind off it." If their grief is on their mind, you won't be able to get it off. Trying to change the topic will make the grieving person feel unheard.

If you feel that the grieving person would be better served by talking to a professional about it, it's helpful to say, "Have you had the opportunity to talk to someone about this?" or even suggest a grief counselor or a support group, if you know of either. If they continue to come to you with heavy talk and sound as though they could use professional support, you may need to encourage them to seek it out.

Don't Take Their Grief On as Your Own

It is hard to see our loved ones suffer. This can create our own grief. But attempting to grieve with them at the same level does nothing to take away their own pain. You can't take grief from someone. You can only be present and witness as they process it themselves. Listen, but let go. After a deep listening session with a grieving person, if you feel unusually heavy energetically, you may want to consider performing a cleansing ritual on yourself to let go of grief that doesn't belong to you. This doesn't make you a selfish support person. Rather, it keeps your own health whole and ultimately makes you a better support person in the long run.

If you find that their situation is triggering your own grief, you may want to seek out your own support, either from a friend or a mental health professional.

If They Are Starting a New Chapter, Be Careful with How You Cheer Them On

If your loved one is grieving the end of a relationship, they may not want to hear how you always thought their significant other was a pile of flaming trash (no matter how true it may be). Avoid playing devil's advocate, even if you think it would be helpful for them to see the other person's side of the story. They may not be in a place to hear that, and again, will feel dismissed. Just listen.

If that person is ready to meet someone else, celebrate that, but avoid trying to usher in someone to replace their former person. They don't need your help creating a dating profile … unless they say that they do! But if they are ready to start dating, don't tell them it's too soon or become overexuberant if they're getting their metaphoric feet wet. Getting out and enjoying the attentions of other people may be a great start to helping them heal from their loss, but the person needs to do it on their own timeline.

Don't Express Your Sorrow at Them for Them to Hold

Maybe their divorce is triggering memories of your own or that of your parents'. Maybe you were super attached to their now-deceased grandmother too. Maybe hearing the stories of how a forest fire ravaged their town reminds you of how scared you are of a hurricane wiping yours away. Your grief is valid, and your loved one's loss may very well be affecting you too. However, it is not the place of the bereaved to comfort you in this time. Turn to people who are further outside the loss (a therapist, a priest/ess/ix, or a friend who is removed from the situation) to comfort you. Your role is to be present for your grieving loved one. It puts an undue burden on them to hold the grief of someone else.

A good model is called the "Ring Theory," developed by clinical psychologist Susan Silk. I strongly encourage everyone to read the original article, a link to which can be found in the footnotes, but a brief overview includes a model of a series of rings. In the center ring is the person experiencing the grief most directly—basically, the person for whom the loss happened. The next ring includes those who are closest to that person, such as spouses, immediate family, etc. The following ring might include close friends, extended family, or others who are connected to the situation but not directly impacted by it. The further out the rings go, the further the people are from the core of the situation. Everyone on the rings may have their own grief process about the loss, but they shouldn't look to people on a ring closer to the center for their comfort. Rather, they must "comfort in" and "dump out."[9] In other words, comfort those who are closer to the situation, and seek comfort from those who are further away from it. This is a healthy model and a way for support people to process their own grief about the situation, while still being respectful to those most directly impacted.

You are not a bad person for having feelings about someone else's loss. The challenge is to work through these feelings in an appropriate context. This will also help you be more present for the person working through a loss.

Be Patient with the Grieving Person

Grieving people are injured people. They may be slow to return your texts or messages. They may be distant when you see them in person. They may flake on their obligations to you or others. They might even do things that seem wildly out of character, such as partying harder, spending a lot of money, or doing other impulsive things.

If you notice them putting themselves in danger or neglecting their needs or the needs of dependents, you or other loved ones may need to encourage them to seek professional help.

---

9. Susan Silk and Barry Goldman, "How Not to Say the Wrong Thing," *Los Angeles Times*, April 7, 2013, https://www.latimes.com/opinion/op-ed/la -xpm-2013-apr-07-la-oe-0407-silk-ring-theory-20130407-story.html.

Be Careful with Cliché Phrases

It's natural to feel some discomfort around a grieving person. It is also natural to want to ease another person's pain. However, cliché sentiments such as "They're in a better place," "Everything happens for a reason," "You'll get over it," "Time heals all wounds," etc. often feel dismissive to a grieving person and generally only feel good to the person saying them. They're easy sentiments and we want them to be true, mostly because we don't want to see our loved ones hurting. However, minimizing a grieving person's suffering, which is what these statements do, makes it worse.

Helpful things to say may include simply, "I am sorry for your loss," "You are in my thoughts," "I love you," or "I'm here." Be intentional with sentiments, acknowledging the grieving person's loss without minimizing it or sweeping it away. Don't force an optimistic stance that the grieving person is unlikely to be ready for.

Remember That Grief Is Not a Problem to Solve

Grief is not a problem at all. It's awful to witness someone you love in grief. It will be very, very tempting to want to fix it for them. But you can't. Even if you could, you shouldn't. Grief is a natural reaction to a painful loss. Your loved one must go through the grief journey on their own. You can listen. You can help them out with tasks and chores. You can certainly pop in to remind them that they're loved and that you're present. But you cannot stop their grief. By treating grief as a problem to solve, you may be unconsciously insinuating that the grieving person is themselves a problem. This might encourage your loved one to stifle their grief around you, which can hurt your relationship. Not only is grief a natural process, it is a human process that they have a right to experience on their own terms.

Stand by. Be present. Remember that grief is not a problem to fix.

Don't Avoid Enjoying Your Life Out of Guilt

Maybe you just got an exciting promotion while your friend is mourning the closing of their business. Maybe you just exchanged "I love you..." for the first time with a new person while a sibling is mourning the death of their partner. Maybe you're about to go on the vacation of your dreams while a good friend is losing a custody battle for their children. Or maybe your life is simply calm and happy while the life of someone you love is riddled with grief. It can feel uncomfortable to celebrate your own joy while knowing someone close to you is suffering so much. Sometimes, we may even feel guilty and want to dampen our own experience. How dare we experience some happiness while someone close to us is struggling so?

However, diminishing your own joy does not reduce the pain for someone else. Grief is not a pie. Adding a slice of grief into your life does not take away pain or grief from someone else. Naturally, you may want to avoid exuberant bubbling over your news to the person who has just lost, but it doesn't mean that you can't be in joy on your own terms. Share your joy with those who are in a good place to hear it, but don't try to minimize your own joy. It doesn't help the griever.

At the same time, the grieving person may feel worse if they're the last one to know about your exciting news. Let's say you got engaged and your best friend is getting divorced. Maybe you don't need to run over and gush about all the details of the engagement— how your partner cried, how much they loved the ring, how your soon-to-be in-laws are throwing you a party, etc. Keep your good news under fifty words or so: "Hey, just wanted to let you know that Rain and I are getting married next year..." It's also okay to let them know you're happy about it. Don't downplay what has happened in your life for their sake. They'll likely know you're doing that and may probably feel the worse for it. Keep them loosely in the loop, but don't let the grieving person be the primary one to get all the exciting details while they are trying to process a major loss of something similar (or not).

Then again, there may be days when your grieving loved one will *want* every detail of your good news. Maybe it gives them hope. Maybe it's a welcome distraction. Maybe they just love you and are genuinely happy for you. But let them be the one to ask how the amazing new thing is going, and at some point, consider saying to them, "I'm happy to share, but please let me know if you don't feel like hearing about it."

Things Witches Should Not Do

Witches who want to help grieving people may be tempted to do some of the following things. If you identify as a Witch and are tempted to do any of the following, please read this next section before doing so ... and consider doing something different to help your grieving loved one!

Do Not Send a Grieving Person an Unsolicited Divinatory Reading about Their Loss

Hence, my story above!

Witches may like to fix things, but such things require consent. If you're absolutely dying to do divination on a grieving person's situation, make it more about you. Consider doing a reading, with whatever medium you use, about how you can best support the person who is grieving.

Be Careful With "Messages"

Well-meant "messages" can be extremely hurtful. For example, don't run to tell the grieving person that you received a message for them from their deceased loved one, or slide into their inbox with a spiritual "download" about their breakup. If the person is grieving someone who passed away, they miss them terribly, and the thought of someone else getting to hear from them is devastating. Unrequested "downloads" about any situation can create confusion and more sorrow. Again, you may firmly believe that your message and information is true and helpful, but it can feel like a slap unless the grieving person has specifically said that they want to hear such messages. (They typically do not.)

I'll admit it: I've been guilty of this. These messages may have been my own mind processing the loss, or perhaps I have received actual visits. Either way, I didn't realize how painful the act was until I was on the receiving end of it. The messages or "downloads" I've received from Witches about my losses have never been accurate. The messages were never things my lost loved ones would have ever said, and the downloads included details irrelevant to my situation.

Now, I do believe I have had visits from deceased people who have living spouses or immediate family members. I also believe there may be some rule that prevents the recently dead from contacting their closest people in this realm. Perhaps it upsets the living too much or makes it difficult for the deceased to move on to their next chapter. I would be lying if I said that there aren't times when I am so energized by the connection with these departed souls that I'm tempted to share my experience with their living people, but I don't for several reasons:

One, my experiences with the departed are about me, not about their living people. I might drop a line to the living person closest to them that simply says, "Hello! Thinking of you!" But I do not mention the encounter with their lost loved one. It signals to my deceased friend that their loved ones are still cared for, and it signals to the bereaved that I am there for them.

If you have received a visit from a deceased person and you believe it's a pertinent message that must get to a grieving person, talk to a third party first. Explain what happened and get their thoughts on whether it would be a good idea to share that knowledge with the grieving person. If this isn't possible, consider making a note of the message with a date. If this message must get to the person, the deceased person will make arrangements (through synchronicity or otherwise) for you to deliver the message. If you do find yourself delivering a message from the deceased to a living person, begin with sensitivity, such as saying, "Please stop me if you feel this is upsetting to you, but I had a strange dream that seemed like it might have some meaning for you. Would you like for me to share it?" It gives the grieving person the opportunity to say no, and if in the event that they would like to hear the message, it gives them the chance to say yes!

Do Not Enable Behavior That Is Draining to You or That Is Unhelpful to the Grieving Person

Some grieving people may be desperate to connect with their lost loved one or to find an explanation for why the loss happened. Many people find their way to Witchcraft because of a loss. They may not find enough answers or support in their religions of origin, and their grief might be their entry point to this path. If you are a reader or a psychic and feel comfortable answering their questions, do set firm boundaries not only for yourself but for their sake as well. The greatest risk with divination is not "demonic possession" (as some fear) but obsession. Obsessing over answers or communication can be a distraction from processing grief, and it's not helpful to the person grieving. A good boundary might be to allow one reading or session every few months for this person. Do encourage them to take time between readings or sessions if they decide to seek counsel from someone else.

Performing Magick for the Grieving

Whether a Witch should perform magick for a grieving person or not raises similar questions to whether or not a Witch should perform magick on someone without their explicit permission. They are both controversial questions. For me, the choice is rooted in context. In general, I want a person's permission before I practice magick on them because I want their cooperation. I don't want to waste my time and energy by doing magick on someone who might inadvertently (or intentionally) subvert my work. However, in situations where I've needed to banish someone or protect myself or others from an intrusive force, I don't seek permission before doing the work, as in those cases, I don't believe permission is warranted.

It is generally best to do magick on the griever if they request the magick themselves or grant you permission if you ask to do it. How each person grieves and what support they want are deeply personal. The kind of magick a grieving person may (or may not) want will be just as subjective. Some people might welcome warm, happy vibes offered by another Witch, while others will want a spell to help them release sorrow. Getting permission before performing magick on a grieving person will not only be respectful of their needs, it also sets the spell up for the greatest success.

If you are offering to help a grieving person with magick, begin by asking, "What would you find helpful right now?" If they can articulate their need, do your best to offer exactly what they ask for, even if you think something different would better benefit them. You can refuse to do the spell if you are too strongly opposed to their desire, but remember that the journey is their own. And if you do the magickal working for them, perform it as closely in line with their wants as possible.

A Spell to Help a Grieving Person

If they welcome the magickal help but don't know what they want, here is a suggested spell:

Print a picture of the grieving person, or simply write their name on a piece of paper. Surround the paper with gentle herbs such as lavender or mint. Outside of the herbs, create a circle with a series of hard stones. A handful of small pieces of obsidian are great to use, but you can also use gravel from a parking lot. If this person is dealing with painful pressure and needs a little more buffering between themselves and the outside world, you may want to create a stronger outer circle, such as using broken glass, a piece of barbed wire, or nails. Make sure the sharp edges are pointed outward (toward the outside world) and not toward the person needing support. This outer circle is meant to protect the person from insensitive or unkind people who might disrupt or aggravate their grieving process.

Light a stick of incense with a gentle scent and waft the smoke over the picture or name of the person. If you can't create smoke in the place where you live or practice, or simply don't want to, sprinkling a little warm water on the picture or name of the person will work fine too.

Say an incantation that creates a space of protected comfort for the grieving person, one that specifies protection from unhelpful outside forces. If you are struggling to find the words, feel free to use this incantation below (or put your own spin on it):

> *Rains of healing, breath of peace,*
> *Bestow a quiet space upon [their name],*
> *Where they may cry and breathe and rest and be,*
> *Until such a time as they may walk on their own again,*
> *Within this space, let their healing begin.*

Periodically check in with the person for whom you're doing the work. It's not good to leave them in this space perpetually, as it's too restrictive and can prevent them from forming new relationships and having new experiences. If they say they are beginning to feel better, let them know you're going to ease the spell.

Begin by removing the protective barrier, leaving the rest of the spell for about three days. After three days, burn the rest of the spell (if you're able) outside, allowing the smoke to be carried away with the wind. If you are not able to burn outdoors, bury the paper in a natural place and declare the spell finished, adding that you are no longer at the helm of this person's healing. It's good to help for a brief time, but it's not good to be connected to this person's grieving process indefinitely. For both their sake and yours, they will need the space to move on and heal on their own.

Hey, Witch, Go Easy on Yourself

You will make mistakes while trying to support a grieving person. Notice that I said *will*, not *might*. You *will* make mistakes. Every loss is different, every grief process unique, and needs within each loss will change. Just as you are trying to figure out how to best be there for your grieving beloved, they are also undergoing a process of understanding their needs in their post-loss world.

Just as hugging someone with a physical wound might elicit an *ouch*, you might accidentally cause an *ouch* when interacting with a grieving person. Metaphorically speaking, listen to the injured person on how to best touch them (or not) while they are healing. Recognize that your attempt to help them might also provoke a metaphoric *ouch* moment. *When* it happens, don't berate yourself or put the grieving person in the position of having to comfort you over your mistake. Simply apologize, but even better, thank them, such as saying something like, "Thank you. I appreciate you letting me know how best to support you."

Even if the grieving person wants space and solitude, it is possible to support them. You can always offer a prayer or energetic intention that says, "May they have what they need to get through this time." There will be trial and error when it comes to helping someone, and just as grieving people deserve patience, kindness, and compassion, so do you. Be sure to save some of that patience, kindness, and compassion for yourself as well.

10
Grief Magick

Six years ago, my husband and I packed our New York apartment into a moving truck, bundled our cats into carriers, and flew across the country to start our lives anew (or for me, renewed) in Oregon. The move had its own grief, even though it was a change we wanted. A better job, being closer to family, and potentially owning a home were on the horizon. But behind us was a big, tight-knit community of friends we loved and a slew of memories. But processing the natural grief of leaving one place for another, even if that's the path we want, would need to wait. Unbeknownst to us, a different loss was coming... but an old friend would warn me.

Two nights after we moved into our new apartment, I sat straight up on the air mattress, livid at a deceased friend named Don. Don died several years before our move to Oregon, and although our friendship was not without its complications (as is common with many friendships between Witches), there was no animosity between us when he passed. But in my dream that night, he was dressed all in black, telling me something I did not want to hear. I woke shaking with fury at my old friend, although I could not remember what he said. But as the day went on, I forgot about the dream.

The next night, my husband and I came home to find our beloved cat Lilith extremely ill. We rushed through the rain to take her to an emergency vet, winding through dark, unfamiliar country roads as fast as our moving van would take us. At the clinic, the veterinarian ran tests and gave us options, but most only offered to prolong our poor cat's suffering rather than cure the tumor we then learned was in her stomach. Just as my husband whispered to me that we needed to talk, I remembered the dream about Don.

Don was a huge cat lover. Many years before, it was while he and I were having dinner that we found Lilith, then a homeless kitten living on a restaurant porch. He encouraged me to adopt her, taught me the basics of cat care, and fed her when I traveled. When our friendship drifted apart because of conflict and eventually distance, I believed he missed Lilith more than me. On that awful night while Lilith, hooked to scary machines, howled in pain and fear, I realized that Don's message in the dream was that my precious cat's time had come to an end. I didn't need to discuss any further treatment options with the vet. I knew Don was present and would help bring her to the next realm.

In the years since, Don has visited me in dreams just prior to someone passing away. He came in a dream the night the mother of one of my closest friends passed away. He even came the night before Anne Rice died (as we shared a passion for her), notifying me that the author was gone before I read the news online. He also came to me just before we lost our pregnancy. Only then, he wasn't alone.

A couple of years ago, as I was writing my Morrigan book, a friend whom I'll call Josh passed away. My grief over Josh was rooted in fury at the world for taking someone so young (he was in his mid-thirties), but also fury at myself for not mending a division between us until just before he passed, missing out on many years of friendship. Worst of all, he had a family. I cried nightly for his young children, who would grow up without their father. The night before we lost our pregnancy, both Josh and Don appeared in the same dream. Don was silent and wouldn't look at me. Josh hugged me. "I've missed you so much!" I remember saying to him. "But I'm doing great! I'm pregnant!"

"I know," Josh said in the dream, with a confusing sadness.

The next day, we lost the pregnancy.

It's possible that these dreams are a trick of evolution. Perhaps there is an innate power within human beings to know when a death is coming—a survival tactic on a planet for which our bodies (without fur, scales, claws, the ability to run fast or see well) aren't particularly well-equipped. Perhaps deep down I knew that my child was dead, and this knowledge manifested in my psyche as visits from dead friends. Or maybe the dead have an easier time reaching me when I sleep. I guess it doesn't matter.

While these experiences are deeply laced with grief, the magick that accompanies them can be a balm. It can be unnerving to think that a dead person has paid you a visit, whether in dreams or in waking life. However, it is often these kinds of encounters that lead many of us to Witchcraft, whether to better understand the unseen world or better harness its power. These experiences can be comforting too. I appreciated the possibility that Don might be there to help our little cat through the surely terrifying process of dying. It was also comforting to think that I might have people on the other side who were there to support my heart when my body seemed to betray me.

A Practice to Build an Otherworldly Network

Just as the grief process is unique, the process of building a magickal practice before, during, and after loss will be deeply personal. Your process and system won't look like mine or anyone else's. You may ask yourself if you're "doing it right," but the only way to verify if a process is right is if it works. Essentially, did it work? Then it worked! Often, once we think we've figured out a process with the spirits, things change again. The best thing to do is to take note in advance and reflect in retrospect.

Basically: notice, notice, notice.

Our world keeps us busy and our attentions divided. For this reason, journaling is crucial. You do not need to be an avid writer or even complete large entries. Your journal can be a series of notes. If you can find a small notepad or book that is small enough to tuck in your bag or purse, that's a good start. Make note of odd encounters with people, animals, or otherwise. Note who or what you dream about. Make a note if you suddenly think of a friend or relative whom you haven't seen or spoken to in years. It's perfectly fine if your journal entries simply say, "Dreamed about Aunt Bertie last night…" or "Saw a coyote on my way to work." Be sure to date the entries.

Try this practice for at least a month. When a loss eventually happens, flip through entries recorded on the days prior to the loss. Who showed up in your dreams? What memories popped up? Did you have odd encounters with animals? Notice patterns and synchronicity, as this is the beginning of you developing communication with the other world. Again, your communication and process will be unique to you, although you may find some patterns mirror things that happened in your family, cultural legacy, or a spiritual tradition you inherited or adopted.

A Practice to Be Open to Receiving Messages

If after doing the work above for a month or more you're still finding that messages are confusing or unclear, you can consider doing the following ritual (with or without your own modifications) to open yourself to other messages from the spirit world.

First, collect a little soil. You won't need much. A pinch from your yard or a nearby park will work just fine. It may be tempting to try to collect soil from places where your ancestors hailed from, but be mindful of the region when taking soil. Areas with heavy tourism, such as Ireland, Greece, or Egypt, experience a great deal of damage from tourists who want to collect soil and rocks from these lands to keep as souvenirs, which is harmful to the lands and historic sites. Even in our most earnest desire to connect with ancestral homelands, it's better to be mindful of the land rather than take from it. Be especially mindful of ecologically sensitive areas, such as areas regenerating after volcanic activity, fires, or landslides. The land will need every piece it can have to regenerate.

Once you've chosen a suitable collection location, make sure you have a container in which to bring the soil back with you. Avoid sweeping dirt or soil from the sidewalk or road, as doing so has other magickal connotations and may have stronger connections to the people who have passed by than the land itself. That kind of work is perfectly usable in other magickal contexts, but not especially for this! While there is no specific protocol for the gathering of soil, you may want to consider making an offering in return of service, such as removing trash or invasive species from the area. Other great land offerings include water (especially if your area is experiencing a drought), singing a song, or simply complimenting the land by telling it how beautiful it is. Everyone likes to know they look good... even land spirits!

Next, select a helpful herb. If you have a favorite herb that you feel brings you closer to the spirit world, collect a piece. If you don't have an herb you like for this, here are some options you can explore. Many of the following herbs relate to ancestry, and the herbs will have familiarity with the work because of their historic use.

- Hollyhock (*Alcea rosea*): Other similar plants include mallow, marsh mallow, or rose of Sharon. In some Hoodoo traditions, keeping the root or leaves of this plant in a jar or next to a bowl of water will attract helpful spirits.[10] These plants are easily gathered in yards or parks.

- Lavender (*Lavandula*): If possible, a fresh sprig is preferable. It's even better if it's one you grew yourself! In a pinch, dried lavender works just fine. When working with dried plants, take time to gently rub the plant and whisper to it to "wake it up." Let it know you have work for it to do and explain that you need it for a magickal working.

---

10. Catherine Yronwode, *Hoodoo Herb and Root Magic: A Materia Magica of African-American Conjure* (Forestville, CA: Lucky Mojo Curio Company, 2002), 28.

- Dandelion (*Taraxacum officinale*): Maybe the world's most friendly little flower, dandelion is great for connecting with spirits. If we can imagine that their sweet little floating seeds can travel across the world carrying our wishes when we blow on them, we can also imagine that their petals, leaves, and even seeds would do the same with our intention to connect with the spirit world.

- Marigold (*Tagetes*): Native to most of South and Central America, the marigold flower is revered in many Latin American countries as a flower with the ability to connect with the ancestors or others in the spirit world. If your ancestors would have recognized this flower as such, this could be a great plant for you to explore. Many people who are not of Latin American descent may have concerns about using this plant in their magick out of fears of cultural appropriation (that is, misusing something from a different culture, or inappropriately "taking" from it). It's a rightful consideration and a much bigger discussion than is within the scope of this book. But for these purposes, it may be helpful to simply ask, "Would my ancestors recognize it?" For myself, if I were to offer marigolds as part of my own spiritual connection, my ancestors would be more likely to think, "Wow! What a pretty orange flower!" than "Oh! Courtney is looking to open communication with us," given that marigolds simply aren't part of my people's traditional ancestral veneration.

If you aren't sure where your ancestors came from or it doesn't feel right using plants that aren't part of your own lineage or tradition, consider embracing dandelion or lavender, which are more universal plants at this point. Even better, consider asking the plants themselves who would like to help you. You may find that a sweet little weed creeping through the sidewalk cracks is eager to assist.

Before harvesting or using any herbs or plants, do research to ensure these are not toxic to humans or pets. Take care also to make sure that any plants you collect are not threatened or endangered. A good plant identifier app can help you identify plants to determine if they are a protected species or potentially dangerous to people or animals if collected and brought into a home. Also, be aware that many parks, roadsides, and empty lots are sprayed with chemicals and pesticides. If you can't collect an herb or plant that you are confident is safe, it may warrant growing your own on a windowsill! In a pinch, it's fine to purchase an herb (fresh or dried) from the grocery store.

Once you have your herb and your soil (if you are using it), create a special space just for these items. If you have an altar, great. A nightstand or kitchen table is fine too. If you're able to burn candles and incense in your home or magickal space, include either or both. Any color of candle is fine. Frankincense, copal, or myrrh incense are particularly helpful to enhance potential spirit world connection.

When you're ready, light the candle and incense, if you are using them. Place the herb in a bowl of water next to the soil. Summon supportive spirits using any incantation you like. If you don't have one, here is one you can use:

Friend and ally,
Here I rally,
For those who wish to warn me, guard me, aid me,
I open the door to your guidance and wisdom.

At this point, consider including a statement about how you might like the messages to come to you. For example, "Come to me in a dream that doesn't frighten me" or "Use the appearance of [x, y, z animal] to catch my attention."

Be sure to thank the spirits for their guidance in advance. Carry the soil in an amulet or a pouch in your wallet, or return it to the earth near the front door of your house. If you live in an apartment, place it near the front door of your building, but before you do, take a finger-full and brush it across the front door of your apartment so the spirits know exactly where to go when they come to visit with messages.

If you have any wards or protective entities already guarding your home, make sure you talk with them and let them know new "faces" may be appearing and to grant them access. This will avoid conflict amongst the spirits.

Of the Spirits That Come to Your Aid, Some May Only Help You Temporarily

Don't be surprised or dismayed if you find that a spiritual ally seems to disappear after a time or even after a single visit. Their disappearance does not mean that you did something wrong. There is likely some sort of protocol in the spirit world that we have no way of confirming or understanding, which might prevent them from sticking around for long. Some may not want to.

It may be tempting to use this work to connect with a recently deceased person, but use caution. Especially if you were particularly close to this person in life or if you are grieving them deeply, it may be difficult or impossible to connect with them. Frankly, this may be for the best. A recently deceased person is working through their transition to the other side, and connecting with the people they were close to in life might make this transition difficult for them. If you are processing the grief over ending a romantic relationship or friendship with someone still living, it's not advisable to try to connect to the spirit guides of those individuals. Their own emotional process, and certainly yours, will complicate the grief process, leaving everyone further tied to the situation. A better practice involves asking for help from spirits who are not connected to the situation or loss themselves but who have experienced similar losses. Not only are they objectively better equipped to help the situation, this will also give you the space to properly grieve and heal.

Identifying Animal Omens

Since the beginning of humankind, the appearance of certain animals has served as omens and messages for the living. Different animals have offered different meanings among different cultures. It is my belief that these traditions grew out of individual encounters, stories of which eventually transformed into folklore and tradition. With this in mind, our own personal associations with certain animals are every bit as strong as those from older traditions. But identifying animal omens can be confusing. An internet search will likely tell you that any animal you see represents "transformation," "growth," or "protection." While this may be true for specific individuals, it's generally watered-down, wishful thinking. If we interpret every animal appearance as a message to make us feel good about our choices, we are missing out on a powerful legacy of animals providing difficult or even terrifying truths.

Here Are a Few of My Own Experiences

One day, I was walking my dog and a turkey buzzard flew low over my head. A little further down on our walk, another turkey buzzard startled my dog and me when it flew out of the bushes, just inches away from us. Buzzards feed on dead things, and seeing two in such close proximity was a clear death omen to me.

I live close to a lot of farms where things die regularly, including rats, mice, deer, etc. Turkey buzzards love those nasty carcasses and appear so frequently that if I were to take every appearance of a turkey buzzard as a sign of incoming loss, I would walk around terrified and also miss the actual omens. In this case, it was the unusually close encounters with these birds that delivered the omen, not the appearances themselves. My assumption was correct. Within twenty-four hours, I received word that two different friends had passed away that week.

The other omen came from a feather. Many modern Witches and Pagans receive appearances of feathers as gifts from the land spirits, and in some cases, I believe that too. But there was one incident that I didn't feel so great about. It was on my birthday, and I was walking through the backyard when I saw a perfect blue jay feather right in my path. The fact that it was on my birthday and directly in my path made me think this wasn't just a feather. Could it have been a birthday present from the spirit world? Maybe. But the blue jay is a serious bully, and I don't trust gifts from bullies. I did some research.

After digging through several "it means transformation…" interpretations on the internet, I found one that chilled my blood. In one Southern African American folk story, the blue jay is a trickster who goes to see the devil every Friday to tattle on the sins of humanity. To see one on a Friday is particularly ominous.[11] While I am not African American, my roots are deep in the American South, and many of my family's own folk practices around luck, health, and protection are heavily influenced by Southern African American culture. Most of all, the day I saw the feather was indeed a Friday. The feather wasn't a gift; it was a warning. Sure enough, within a few weeks, the deadly fires that scarred Oregon's landscape arrived—their own form of hell. The spirits were very clear.

Just as you will want to avoid assuming that every animal you see is bringing good news and transformation, avoid assuming that every animal you encounter represents an impending loss, as that can create unnecessary anxiety. And just as you may take note of strange dreams or odd moments, take note of unusual circumstances with an animal. For example, did one cross your path particularly closely? Did you lock eyes with the creature? Was the animal an unusual one for your region? Look back on these notes later and watch for patterns. The clarity of the message may take years to emerge, but even with a long journey, it's a worthwhile practice and valuable tool.

A Few Rituals

A ritual for every type of loss would quickly fill up its own book. As with all of the practices in this book, this section lends itself to wide interpretation. Use these as inspiration, not prescription. Let yourself feel empowered to make changes and personalize them as you see fit, particularly if your specific loss is different than one of the ones described below.

---

11. Newman Ivey White, ed., "Jaybirds, Mockingbirds, Filliloo Birds," *The Frank C. Brown Collection of North Carolina Folklore*, vol 7, part 2, *Popular Beliefs and Superstitions from North Carolina* (Durham, NC: Duke University Press, 1943), 394–95.

A Ritual for the Ending of a Romantic Relationship

If this is the end of a relationship and the person is still living, it may prove helpful to begin by returning their possessions and removing things from your sight that remind you of them.

Take an image of the two of you (or more, if this is a polyamorous dynamic). Anoint a pair of scissors with a mixture of salt, water, and apple cider vinegar. Slice your image away from theirs, turning their face(s) down but your face up. If the tears fall, let them. A suggested incantation is as follows:

> *I walk alone, I walk free,*
> *Whether or not my desire, so mote it be.*
> *My heart is broken, but mine it is still,*
> *I take the pieces and fold to my will.*

At this time, it may be helpful to speak to the image of your beloved(s). Tell them what's on your heart, whether it's kind or cruel or angry, or even unfair in your mind. Don't worry about if you're being "unfair" or "irrational." You are speaking to the representation of the person or people you are grieving. Their feelings will not be hurt, nor will they retaliate in anger. This is for your healing.

Don't rush to dispose of the image of the other person or people. Repeat this ritual as often as you would like. Your communication with the image may change from day to day. Some days you may feel more anger, other days more sadness. This ritual is appropriate even when you are the one who chose to end the relationship.

You'll know that the ritual is complete when you feel the air is cleared between you and the person or people, and you no longer feel as though there is something left unsaid. At this point, thank the image for holding the space and let it know its job is done. Dispose of the picture in a gentle way. It can be buried or even placed in the garbage.

If after a period of time you feel you need to redo the ritual, go for it! Download or print out a new image of the person or people you are grieving and do the whole thing again. Don't be hard on yourself if the grief returns even years later. Remember, it's a spiral and not a line!

A Ritual for the Loss of a Friend

Friendship loss is strongly underrated as a powerful space of grief. Some may argue that it can be more painful and last even longer than that of a romantic partner.

Take a yellow rose to an outdoor space, if possible. If this is a locally grown rose, even better, as it has a small carbon footprint. (Do not use plastic flowers for this ritual.) The outdoor space can be your yard, a park, or another area. Sit with the rose and reflect on all the things you miss about your friend (whether or not you chose to leave the friendship). Again, tears are fine and encouraged if they feel right.

Remove one petal from the rose at a time, and with each petal, speak to something that you miss about the person. Release each petal to the ground. (This is a great ritual to do on a windy day, as the wind will catch the rose petals.)

Alternative: Speak to the rose daily in a similar ritual to the one above. As the rose wilts, it holds the messages. Release to the yard waste bin or garbage when you're ready.

A Ritual for the Loss of an Enemy

Losing someone with whom you had a complicated or antagonistic relationship is also an under-discussed form of grief. Very often, enemies are people we once loved. Sometimes, they were people who betrayed us or whose irreconcilable differences were just too much. We may grieve because they didn't get what we feel they deserved in life and may have gone to their grave without facing, in our mind, proper justice. We may have longed for an opportunity to mend the rift and won't get it. It's possible we may even feel celebratory about their loss, or even a mix of feelings. The death of an enemy is bound to bring up extremely complex emotions and a very unusual experience of grief. It's all valid. Part of most Western death culture involves speaking only good of the dead when they pass, but if we do not feel a person was good or if we only had poor or hurtful experiences with them, there may be a need to speak into that. It can also be hard to watch people grieve someone whose death did not affect you as sad. There may even be relief on your part for this loss. Again, all of this is valid.

If you are processing the death of an enemy, you can replicate the ritual for the loss of a romantic relationship, but instead, say the things that you wanted to say in life that you didn't get a chance to, particularly if these are angry or even mean things that might not be received well by people who are in active grief over the person's loss. As with the ritual above, this can be repeated as many times as you'd like over as long as you'd like.

At some point, the grief process can gift you the freedom of no longer having this person in your life. At that point, you may want to rip or shred the image of the person, and when you do so, here is an incantation you can say:

Thread from thread, limb from limb,
Your power over me is at an end.
Weep no more for this life lost,
My soul and heart bear not the cost.
The death knell calls,
Tears shall not fall.

Of course, you may have more tears for this situation, and so this incantation is not to stop the grief process from taking its course, but to declare that your own struggle and sorrow over this presence in your life is at an end.

If you are concerned that this is a person who may come back to haunt you, you can weave that intention into the above incantation as well, including a phrase such as, "No more shall we meet; me in my life you shall not seek." You may also want to consider asking a trusted spirit guide, ancestor, saint, or deity to protect you. Some people take troll, goblin, or gargoyle figures and place them on either side of their front door. In the former cases, while you will want to make regular offerings, these beings are used to this kind of work and are unlikely to be surprised by the ask. For the latter, which are more earthbound spirits with a little less familiarity, you'll want to do regular devotions and instructions for them, including describing the person you want to keep out of your house and life. Regularly walking the boundaries of your property, house, or apartment to declare this space as yours and that no one who can cause harm can enter will certainly be helpful as well.

A Ritual for the Grief over the Loss of a Pet

Losing a pet is one of the most underrated and underexplored forms of grief. For thousands of years, humans have been in close relationship with animals—relying on them for survival; meat, fur or wool, or protection, as well as companionship. Witches frequently form powerful, spiritual bonds with their animals. Sometimes, they even see the animals as a "familiar," which is currently most commonly understood to be an animal with whom the Witch has a spiritual bond and may even assist, in their own way, in magickal work. For many years, my cat Lilith would join the rituals I did; she would walk around the magickal objects in play or would stand beside whoever was speaking at the time. She wasn't the friendliest cat and generally preferred to be left alone by everyone, but when magick began, she wanted to be a part of it. The day we lost her was like having something carved out of my heart.

It's not "just an animal." Remember, we humans have bonded with animals for thousands of years. The grief over losing an animal with which we are bonded is every bit as real as losing a human person with whom we are bonded, by blood or by heart. For some of us, it may be even more painful, and yet the world does not stop to allow us to grieve our animals in the way that it generally allows us to grieve humans. As a measure of helping yourself in the time after losing a pet, don't shy away from having a memorial service or some other kind of funerary ritual for your animal. Feel empowered to invite people to join you, if you would like, to mourn the passing of your beloved companion. Doing so also normalizes the grief process over losing the animal for others.

While in your sacred space, either on your own or with others, talk to your animal's spirit. Let them know how much they were loved, and if you had to euthanize them, explain why it needed to happen. Chances are, they understood, but you may find it comforting to say the words aloud. Particularly empathetic animals may struggle to cross over spiritually, so do let them know that although you will miss them terribly, you will be all right. A practice my husband and I have utilized when we've had to say goodbye to our pets is to let them know they are welcome to return whenever they want. As always, here is an incantation you can use if you are struggling for words or if you simply want to say something a little different:

> *My precious friend, my heart in [fur, feathers, or scales],*
> *Be released and now be free,*
> *From suffering, fear, cold, or want.*
> *May we meet, know, and love again.*

Other things you can do to honor your pet:

- If your animal was cremated, place their ashes on your ancestor altar. You can also include their collar, tags, or beloved toys.
- Donate to an animal shelter or rescue in their name.
- Plant flowers or trees near where you may have buried them or their ashes.
- Volunteer for a cleanup event at their favorite park.

A Ritual When Unable to Say Goodbye

The need to say goodbye and create some sort of closure is deeply human. As we explored, the need for closure is so frequently masked as wanting answers, but it's more often that answers will not happen. While we cannot create answers, we can certainly create the opportunity to say goodbye. The pandemic left us unable to attend many funerals, denying people the human need to say goodbye.

"Ghosting" someone (when someone disappears from your life without an explanation) is not new. When my husband and I were having construction work done on our house, we found a box of old letters from a hundred years ago. One letter was from a teenaged girl to her boyfriend (who had presumably kept the letter), saying goodbye to him as he had stopped writing to her. We can blame dating apps and online blocking as a culprit in ghosting, but these old letters proved that the act of disappearing on someone—whether a friend or a romantic partner—rather than definitively ending it, is not new.

Whether this person has passed away or remains alive but is no longer in your life, you may find it helpful to create a goodbye ritual of your own. Here is one suggestion:

Write them a letter on plain paper, listing all of the things that were left unsaid. Feel free to express your rage, hurt, anger, and more. Take the time to also think about the things that you appreciated about your time with them: the way you used to laugh together, something they taught you, something you unwittingly learned from them. If the page fills up, write over your words at the beginning.

Soak the piece of paper in a bowl of salt water, "smushing" the paper until it begins to dissolve.

If possible, light four candles around the bowl. Any color is fine, but for this one, I would recommend white candles. Battery-operated candles are fine too.

Depending on your region, start with north. You may have different versions of what constitutes the different areas of north, south, east and west. For this example, I will be using the associations most often seen in the Northern Hemisphere, but again, move them around to adjust to your surroundings. For each of the candles, recite the following (or a version of the following):

Candle in the north:

The foundations of our time together may crumble, but the memory resides in my heart. I release myself and you from ice and rock and bone. Be released from our time and place together. Hand upon hand, and flesh upon flesh. I release, release, release.

Candle in the west:

The waters that be, wash away that which binds us together in time and place but not in heart or memory. Releasing the gates to the west, may you go and flow freely. I release, release, release.

Candle in the south:

Fire to purify, heat to warm. May the warmth of the sun and the heart of the earth guide your way and protect you as you go along. While we two part, the warm memory remains. I release, release, release.

Candle in the east:

Open the gates to the brightening dawn. Let the new light in, let the new come forth. New days for us both, in this realm or the next. I release, release, release and welcome the breath of the new way.

In this final section of the ritual, if there are any words you'd still like to say, say them now. They do not have to be "nice." They can be harsh or whatever you need them to be.

On the final part of the ritual, extinguish each candle, saying one final goodbye with each extinguishing. It's important to extinguish the candles yourself before they burn all the way out. This is important for the final goodbye.

When the paper is nearly or fully dissolved, dispose of it and the water outside, away from your home.

11
The Myth of "Getting Over It"

I have good news for you. You won't "get over it."

Wait, what? You may ask. That sounds like terrible news! I don't want to grieve forever!

Well, I have more good news!

You won't grieve forever. At least, not as you are grieving now. Grief will shift and ease. There will come a time when your life no longer feels controlled by it. But the good news about not "getting over it" is that because you won't ever "get over it," you don't have to *try* to get over it. You're also not going to sprout wings and fly or pop gills and breathe underwater. You don't have to waste your time envisioning feathers growing out of your arm or will yourself to grow gills, and not doing so won't mean you're a failure. And since you're not going to "get over" your loss, you're not a failure at that either.

No one truly "gets over" a loss. Instead, we adjust to a new way of being. If we've been lying in the dark and someone suddenly turns the lights on, the light hurts at first, but then our eyes adjust. If the lights suddenly turn off, we may be disoriented in the sudden darkness, but then again, we adjust. When we jump into a cold body of water, it is a shock at first, but then we adjust. Grief is like that. On the other side of loss, we learn a new way of being.

I didn't get over my high school friends' deaths, but my life did continue. I don't linger under the sadness that I had in those early days, yet to say my life hasn't been shaped by their deaths would be a lie. Nothing went back to "as it was" before their deaths. The world was different, and that old world, the one prior to their loss, was gone. This loss has been a guiding force in my decision-making, for better or worse, and shaped how I see life. I learned very early how finite the flesh experience is for all of us, and how suddenly and randomly we might each leave this world. Sometimes, a deep and hard sadness still hits me, such as when I see pictures of their permanently young faces or connect with old classmates whose lives have also been indelibly shaped by the loss.

I am happy in my marriage and am truly thankful that my last relationship fell apart. But there are times when I see a funny meme or run into a mutual friend, and I wish I could text the person whose friendship meant so much to me before we tried romance. I don't miss this person as a lover, but I do miss my old friend. For me, grief over losing that friendship has lasted longer than that of the romance. And although a drive or hike through the charred trees of my state's formerly beautiful forests hurts, the lush, green growth blooming at the base of the blackened tree trunks gives me hope.

Plus, as I write this, in roughly six weeks, I'm due to give birth to my daughter. She's expected to arrive just a few days after what would have been my last baby's first birthday. Given both dates' proximity to Imbolc, it's possible that Brigid has been with me this whole time.

There is a lot of joy in a healthy, advanced pregnancy, but also a lot of fear. I have recurrent nightmares of loss. Decorating the nursery and receiving beautiful gifts from friends is exciting, but these things also plant a large fear behind my heart: What if I have to return these things? And the love I feel for my unborn child doesn't mean I don't feel the absence of the child I lost. But these days, I feel more joy and hope than sorrow and despair. Love, joy, optimism, and appreciation for the way things ultimately worked out: none of those erase the pain of loss, and none of them neutralize grief. In time, grief does not minimize or neutralize joy either. Grief and joy can and will exist simultaneously.

With time, joy will take the lead.

Can We Choose Healing?

Time can do wonderful things for us. It can bring new blessings, it can help us adjust, and in time, we can function in our new way of being. But the phrase "Time heals all wounds" is false. Healing a physical injury takes time, and it also takes choice. A physical injury may need medicine and occupational therapy as part of its healing process, and taking the necessary medications and performing recommended therapies is itself an act of choice. Likewise, grieving a loss will take time, but at a certain point, it may require choice.

What the choice looks like depends on the nature of the loss and what the person needs. For some, it may be the choice to attend a support group, seek counseling, or even try doctor-prescribed medications. For others, it may be engaging in new activities or moving to a new place. For many, it may be opening the mind to acceptance: accepting that the loss took place, accepting that it was painful, unfair, or unjust, while also accepting that life will not be the same again.

What choosing healing does *not* look like is pretending that everything is okay or that the loss never happened.

Sometimes we may make choices that help us in our new life and find that we're not ready. Like healing a broken ankle, maybe we try taking a walk and find that the ankle just isn't strong enough yet. Maybe we go on a date after losing a partner, thinking we may be ready, and find that it's too painful. Perhaps we attend a concert of a band a deceased loved one adored and find the music makes us hurt.

We back off. We will try again at another time.

Grief Is Not Our Identity

All lives will be affected by grief. We can't prevent loss. We can't rush grief. But we do not have to let our personal stories be solely defined by our loss or losses. Grief does not need to be our identity.

Grief can be like mud, and we can get stuck in it. When everything we experience is seen through the lens of our loss, we prevent ourselves the opportunity to live fully in the blessed moments that will surely come our way after our loss. We can embrace our new world, and our new selves, without minimizing the impact our loss had on us.

But remember, choosing healing is not "getting over it." Getting over it implies that we no longer have feelings about the loss, and that thought just isn't realistic. Choosing healing means we are choosing to continue with our lives and consciously creating more space for joy. It doesn't mean that grief won't raise its voice occasionally, even decades after the loss.

Not everyone will understand that. You may find that some people who were sympathetic in the beginning of your grief journey become impatient. If people start to say unhelpful things such as "It's time to let it go …" or even an unkind, "Get over it," here are some ways you can respond:

"I know you mean well, but I'm working through this on my own timeline."

"'Getting over it' may be part of your process, but your process is different than mine."

"Please give me space and respect my need to heal in my own way."

"I won't be getting over it, thank you. I'm learning to live without what I've lost."

"You may mean well, but those comments are unhelpful, and I ask that you respect my desire not to hear them anymore."

Or devise your own flavor and language.

If there is only one thing you have taken from this book, I hope it is that there are no keys to solving the grieving process. Grief can't be solved because grief is not a problem. Grief is a natural reaction to the human experience of having lost. It's complicated. It's messy. It is also a journey with gifts and opportunities to learn along the way. It doesn't have to make sense. In fact, it probably won't. And that's okay.

Conclusion

Your grief journey will be as unique to you as your Witch journey. I don't have a moment when I returned to Witchcraft after losing the baby, even while getting the good news about the new pregnancy. But I realized that I never stopped being a Witch. Just as I fell back into the relationships my grief had fractured, I fell back into relationship with Witchcraft. But just as those relationships changed, so did my relationship with Witchcraft. When our hearts break, they change. We love differently. But we still love.

Slowly, my Witchcraft practice returned. I lit candles on my altar because it felt good to do so. I began pulling tarot cards for myself and my husband because I appreciated having that time with him, and in time, remembered the magick of why I was drawn to tarot in the first place. I feel closer to my ancestors than I did before this loss, and I appreciate the beauty of the natural world even more. Part of that is taking advantage of the beauty my lost child will never get to experience. It's both a gift to me and an obligation to that child, to keep living because they could not.

One night recently, my husband was inspired to perform a ritual and asked me to join him. He led, I followed—a change of pace for me, who spent nearly a decade leading rituals for giant groups. I walked into the sacred space he created with no intention of my own and teared up at the beautiful familiarity. I don't know what my future as a Witch looks like, but I know that the practice is one thing I have not lost.

For me, being a Witch means embracing mystery. I don't know why things happen, particularly terrible things. If the gods are real and they have the answers, they're not sharing them. Still, I can love these mysteries and appreciate their beauty. If there's any way that I, as a Witch, can navigate loss, this is how.

The journey continues. Some days, it's still hard. Other days are fresh and new, and the loss feels far away. Most days are somewhere in between, but a year past my loss, the hard moments are only sprinkled about here and there. There is far more laughter and joy. I find that I appreciate those joyful moments more now than I did before my loss.

The path of Witchcraft may have called to you because of its unique qualities, its freedom, despite (or because of) there being no road map. There is no road map to grief either. My wish for you is that in these pages you found a few pieces that helped you navigate this journey. No one can walk it completely with you. Your specific journey is yours to carve out, as no one has experienced your grief or loss before. Still, you are following a legacy of souls, all of whom have experienced loss since time began. And for each of them, the opportunity for joy followed, as it will for you as well.

In that, you will never be alone.

Acknowledgments

Neither healing nor writing are solitary journeys, even if they feel that way. This book and journey were many years in the making, and I offer my profound thanks to the Circle of Beloveds who held and supported me through this book's creation and my own healing: Lisa Anderson, gina Breedlove, Josi Davis, Britta Dinsmore, Mónica Divane, Ivo Dominguez Jr., Ryan Easton, Elysia Gallo and the team at Llewellyn Worldwide, Carla Gaskins-Nathan, Renee Hill, Judika Illes, Sue Johnston and the RESOLVE community, Chaweon Koo, Tamsin Langley-Davis, Fio Gede Parma, Keisha McKenzie, Theresa Reed, Tamrha Richardson, Kanani Soleil, Hilary Whitmore, the TWL Squad, my beloved family, and my husband, Brian, who stood beside me once more on the creation of another hard book and a canon of even harder lessons. Finally, to the ones who left, those who stayed, and to those who were taken away.

Bibliography

Boss, Pauline. *The Myth of Closure: Ambiguous Loss in a Time of Pandemic and Change.* New York: W. W. Norton & Company, 2022.

Mapes, Lynda V. "'I Am Sobbing': Mother Orca Still Carrying Her Dead Calf—16 Days Later." *The Seattle Times.* Updated May 13, 2019. https://www.seattletimes.com/seattle-news /environment/i-am-sobbing-mother-orca-still-carrying-her -dead-calf-16-days-later/.

Pollack, Rachel. *Seventy-Eight Degrees of Wisdom: A Tarot Journey to Self-Awareness.* Newburyport, MA: Weiser Books, 2020.

Silk, Susan, and Barry Goldman. "How Not to Say the Wrong Thing." *Los Angeles Times.* April 7, 2013. https://www.latimes .com/opinion/op-ed/la-xpm-2013-apr-07-la-oe-0407-silk-ring -theory-20130407-story.html.

White, Newman Ivey, editor. *The Frank C. Brown Collection of North Carolina Folklore*. Vol. 7, part 2, *Popular Beliefs and Superstitions from North Carolina*. Durham, NC: Duke University Press, 1943.

Yronwode, Catherine. *Hoodoo Herb and Root Magic: A Materia Magica of African-American Conjure*. Forestville, CA: Lucky Mojo Curio Company, 2002.

To Write to the Author

If you wish to contact the author or would like more information about this book, please write to the author in care of Llewellyn Worldwide Ltd. and we will forward your request. Both the author and publisher appreciate hearing from you and learning of your enjoyment of this book and how it has helped you. Llewellyn Worldwide Ltd. cannot guarantee that every letter written to the author can be answered, but all will be forwarded. Please write to:

Courtney Weber
℅ Llewellyn Worldwide
2143 Wooddale Drive
Woodbury, MN 55125-2989
Please enclose a self-addressed stamped envelope for reply,
or $1.00 to cover costs. If outside the U.S.A., enclose
an international postal reply coupon.

Many of Llewellyn's authors have websites with additional information and resources. For more information, please visit our website at http://www.llewellyn.com.